Edith Wharton's
French Riviera

For Arlette Nastat

Editorial Direction by Julie Rouart

Translated from the French by Susan Pickford

Copy-editing and typesetting by Kate van den Boogert

Graphic design by Dune Lunel/Modzilla

Color separation by Eurisis

Originally published as *La Côte d'Azur au Temps d'Edith Wharton*
© 2002 Flammarion
English-language edition
© 2002 Flammarion

ISBN 2-0801-0722-4
FA0722-02-V
Dépôt légal : 05/2002

Printed in Italy

Edith Wharton's
French Riviera

Philippe Collas **Éric Villedary**

Flammarion

5ᵐᵉ Année   Le Nᵒ 0 fr. 25   Saison 1910-11

LE JOURNAL DES ÉTRANGERS

Revue Mondaine Illustrée

PIERRE COMBA

L'ACTUALITÉ	Publiant — la —	LE MONDE

LISTE OFFICIELLE DES HIVERNANTS

de

CANNES

GRASSE

THORENC - VENCE - CAGNES

SAINT-RAPHAËL

LA NAPOULE - THÉOULE - TRAYAS - AGAY

LE CANNET

Paraissant le
Samedi soir

ANTIBES

GOLFE-JUAN - JUAN-LES-PINS

HYÈRES

Ste-MAXIME - St-AYGULF - LE LAVANDOU

LE THÉATRE		LES SPORTS

RÉDACTION	DIRECTION-ADMINISTRATION	ABONNEMENTS
Directeur - Rédacteur en Chef : **ALFRED MARTIN** Secrétaire de la Rédaction : **GASTON DORIAN**	**F. ANDRAU & Cⁱᵉ** ÉDITEURS 10, RUE BOSSU · CANNES · TÉLÉPHONE 6.31	La Saison....... **8** frs. Union Postale.... **10** frs. *Le Numéro* . **0.25**

table of contents

introduction

Edith Wharton at her writing desk
in New York in the 1890s.

introduction

When Edith Wharton discovered the French Riviera she was at a turning point in her life. Recently divorced and getting over a passionate love affair, she was ready for a fresh start. For the first time she felt she had thrown off the shackles of convention and was free to live her life as she desired. At fifty-seven, she finally knew what it was to experience the torments of passion that she had so often described in her books. She at last felt able to say all that she wanted to say, with the satisfaction of drawing on her own private well of experience. Yet curiously, she found that the chaotic love affair that had just ended had not taught her anything that she had not somehow always known. This discovery strengthened her deeply held conviction that the artist does not need to be personally familiar with all aspects of the situation he is describing, and that the true creative soul has an innate knowledge of all human experience. Edith Wharton was happier than she had been for a long time; her confidence in her creative powers was renewed, and life seemed to be smiling on her.

And yet it was 1919. Edith's mentor and friend Henry James had passed away just three years earlier, and the world was still coming to terms with the aftermath of the Great War. Ironically, Edith found freedom just as the old world, the world she had grown up in and written about, that golden age before the war, was swept away forever. She had been through the mills before, however, and now reacted as she always did, by finding a magical, enchanting spot to settle down and make her own, where she could learn to live once again, in peace and harmony. Her deep love of houses and gardens was not a superficial or simply aesthetic interest, but rather the symptom of an absolute need to have roots or a shelter to protect her from life's storms.

Edith Wharton moved to Paris in 1905 shortly after taking French citizenship. The move to the Midi, as the French call the south of France, was really a natural progression. Her new house, the Pavillon Colombe, in the village of St.-Brice-sous-Forêt, just outside Paris, was unfinished, providing the perfect excuse for one of her frequent motoring tours. Holidaying for four months in Hyères on the Côte d'Azur, she experienced a powerful sensation of rebirth. It seemed as if she were made for the Riviera—and the Riviera for her. For the next eighteen years, until her death in 1937, Edith would divide her time, in typical aristocratic style, between her two French properties, spending spring and summer in St. Brice near Paris, and autumn and winter in her château on the Mediterranean coast.

Although—or maybe because—her books are full of shadows, repressed but violent emotions, and inner torments, Edith Wharton always seemed to need to be at the center of a bright social whirl, as a way to balance those darker aspects of her creative side. Like Oscar Wilde and Marcel Proust, she needed the superficial sparkle and glitter of society life to help foster her inner life. Perhaps she also found a reflection of her interior

Edith Wharton on the
terrace of the Grand Hotel
des Îles d'Or in Hyères.

self in the permanent sunshine of the Riviera: wonderful, warming, but also scorching and pitiless for those
unaccustomed to its rays.

And so Edith Wharton, the most English of Americans and the most French of novelists writing in English,
eventually found the haven that had been an almost physical need for her all her life. A woman of the
nineteenth century swept up in the excitement of a new era, she is truly one of the emblems of the magical
French Riviera, a part of the world considered a paradise by the English and Americans who flocked to it in
huge numbers—but of course a paradise must contain its serpents.

In writing this book, a curious parallel has arisen between the story of this dry, sunburned corner of France,
molded by a few wealthy visitors' dreams of Eden, and Edith Wharton's most famous novels. Both are filled
with beauty and cruelty, excesses, drama, and passion. The story of Edith Wharton on the Riviera could very
well be the plot to one of her own novels: it is the story of a society searching for itself.

Villa Île-de-France, St.-Jean-Cap-Ferrat.
Built by the eccentric Béatrice Ephrussi de Rothschild,
the villa was originally constructed in canvas. This
extremely expensive process was designed to give the
beautiful baroness an idea of what her finished home
would look like before it was even built: virtual reality in
1900! The park has seven themed gardens; this
photograph shows the French-style parterre.

the age of innocence
(before 1919)

Vue de Menton, prise du pont Carré. — D'après M. Al. Nègre.

A view of Menton from the Carré Bridge.
Engraving in the style of M. Al. Nègre. Menton was once
an Italian village with a tropical climate; it belonged to
the Grimaldi family—rulers of Monaco—until 1848.

Edith Wharton arrived in the south of France just in time to witness the final years of a brilliant, glittering society of the sort she so often depicted in her novels with a kind of ambiguous fascination. All her life she had lived among America's *nouveaux riches*, and had witnessed their excesses. The society she found in the south of France was an extension of this same lifestyle. On the Riviera, as in Newport, Connecticut, everything seemed possible—even the very landscape could be changed to suit a passing whim. Extraordinary characters would flit through, spending a week or a month dazzling their hosts before moving on to the next gathering of admirers. This microcosm of American life was a never-ending source of fascinating observations for a writer like Edith Wharton, a lifelong student of the *comédie humaine*.

The Côte d'Azur had been "invented" as a holiday spot by a few immensely wealthy Englishmen during the nineteenth century, and by the time Edith herself arrived in 1919 it was home to an entirely self-contained English-speaking society whose motto echoed the advice given to Edith by her mother, "Never speak about money, and think about it as little as possible!" Nothing was too beautiful, too big, too flashy, as long as it helped the eternal holidaymakers forget the burden of mortality.

But what was it precisely about this part of France that cast such a spell? It is hard to say, but between October and March this little strip of coast attracted travelers as if by magic, all following the

example of a few wealthy British pioneers. The tide of luxury that washed over the region every winter was ephemeral, in the way of waves, and every spring the flocks of "winter swallows", as they were prettily termed, would fly away to other climes, covering their furniture in dust sheets and fleeing the burning summer sun. This was the pattern throughout the nineteenth century and the *belle époque*; every summer the region was deserted by the rich families who spent the winter there. The beaches and avenues were left empty, and the locals were free to wander the sleepy roads, past the great houses shuttered up for the summer, waiting for the next winter and the influx of lavish visitors. It is hard for us to imagine such scenes nowadays, accustomed as we are to worshipping the sun.

The Invention of the Côte d'Azur

In the early nineteenth century, the stretch of Mediterranean coast between the towns of Nice and Menton was discovered by English travelers, a number of whom bought properties in the region. Paradoxically, the first visitors were drawn not by the spectacular beauty of the scenery, but rather by the hope of curing that nineteenth-century scourge, tuberculosis. This illness, so closely associated with the Romantic period, killed more people than had all of Napoleon's campaigns. The doctors of the time were powerless against the disease; all they could do

A sanatorium near Nice.
As the Côte d'Azur's warm and dry climate was recommended for tuberculosis patients, a large number of sanatoria were built.

was recommend a change of air. A spell in the Alps or the mild climate of the Mediterranean was the solution, if one could afford it. The British tended to choose the Mediterranean for two reasons. It made a change from their cold, damp climate, but they were also influenced by the Romantic poetry of Lord Byron, a fervent devotee of the region. Soon, hundreds of pale, nostalgic, young invalids were making the trip south, there to spend their fortunes in an effort to beat the disease. They were often obliged to remain for long periods, so their friends and family would visit and discover the joys of the Côte d'Azur for themselves. From this time on, the hotels—which were still few and far between—were fully booked every winter, only emptying again when the burning summer sun returned, sending the visitors scurrying back to cooler climes.

It very quickly became clear that the local facilities were in no way adequate to deal with this seasonal rush of visitors. Although mass tourism was still a long way off, steps were already being taken that would help pave its way. As early as 1823, the Reverend Lewis Way began collecting funds back in England to finance the construction of a decent road along the coast around Nice. This project was designed to give easier access for visitors, but also as a way to provide work for the local population, which at the time was one of the poorest in Italy (at this time the county of Nice formed part of the kingdom of Piedmont-Sardinia, only becoming part of France after a referendum in 1860) and whose farm laborers in particular were reduced to absolute destitution every winter. It was a way of ensuring the locals benefited from the increasing popularity of their region. The inhabitants of Nice called this road *lou camin dei Anglès*, which later became the legendary Promenade des Anglais, or English Promenade, the main avenue along the Nice seafront, where today people come to see and be seen. The town's English-seeming name seemed to predestine it to become the largest English settlement on the continent. As early as 1829, the British consulate in the town counted more than one hundred families who came for the winter every year, each bringing numerous friends and extended family, not to mention servants. In his *Impressions de Voyage*, Alexandre Dumas *père*, the creator of the immortal *Three Musketeers*, tells this charming anecdote about the major part the British played in the life of the region:

For the inhabitants of Nice, all travelers are English: every foreigner, regardless of hair color, beard, clothes, age, and sex, comes from some phantasmagoric town shrouded in fog, where one might hear the sun mentioned once or twice as an ancient tradition, where oranges and pineapples are known only by name, the only ripe fruit are cooked apples, and which in consequence of this is called London. While I was staying at the Hotel d'York, a poste chaise arrived. A moment later, the innkeeper

**The grand entrance to the
casino in Nice** at the beginning
of the twentieth century. The
gambling rooms were a
place to see and be seen.

In the lobby of the Nice Casino, during the
celebrated Nice Carnival, in 1900. From its
inauguration in 1882, the casino was a highly
popular meeting place, frequented by
courtesans and crowned heads alike.

The little port at Cannes.
In the mid-nineteenth century,
Cannes was still a small fishing port.

The Villa Éléonore-Louise.
Its architecture is in the medieval style. It was
one of the first major villas on the Côte d'Azur.

the age of innocence **18**

*came into my room. I asked who the new arrivals
were. "Sono certi Inglesi" he replied, "ma no soprei
dire se sono Francesi o Tedeschi". Which means, "They
are certainly English, but I could not say whether they
are French or German.'*

The year 1834 marked a turning point in British
involvement in the region. The Lord Chancellor,
Lord Brougham, an important and vastly wealthy
man, came to the Côte d'Azur. His beloved daughter
had been diagnosed with consumption, and he was
prepared to do everything within his power to save
her. The pair were unable to enter Nice due to a
cholera epidemic, so they stopped instead in
Cannes, a tiny and completely unknown fishing port.
He was immediately seduced by this charming spot,
and decided to build a fashionable Italian-style villa,
baptized Villa Éléonore-Louise. He spent nearly
thirty-five years there—years that saw great changes
to the little town, as Cannes rapidly became a
favorite holiday spot for the British establishment.
The press was especially enthusiastic, making
extravagant claims for the fishing port,

> *Cannes is the land of sun, the cradle of life; Cannes is
> Madeira without the yellow fever, Corsica without the
> vendettas, Switzerland without the cold, Baden
> without the snow, Italy without the malaria, Greece
> without the thieves, Asia without the plague, Africa
> without the simoom…*

Members of parliament like Sir Temple Leader
and businessmen like Michael Hugh Scott, the cod

liver oil king, flocked to the coast, looking for sun,
and maybe for wealthy clients among the invalids.
They built majestic villas, while the less moneyed
locals had to be content watching all the works in
progress, maybe helping out in exchange for a few
meals. The Scott Château, a type of *faux* medieval
Scottish affair, was the first outpost of a new fashion
for mixing and matching architectural styles, which
soon reigned supreme. Mr. Scott, loyal to the ways of
his native country, lived to an entirely British
rhythm, his days punctuated by the unvarying
ceremony of five o'clock tea. Any adaptation to local
customs was not for him! His home and lifestyle
were that of the Highlands laird in all respects but
one: the brilliant sunshine all year round, which
spoiled the illusion somewhat. His weird and
wonderful château, all Gothic turrets and
crenellations, was visited by the future prime
minister, William Gladstone, and even inspired film
director Marcel L'Herbier for his film *Le Mystère de
la Chambre Jaune.*

When Italy ceded the county of Nice to France in
1860, the region underwent a renewed period of
economic development, which meant in particular
that the Côte d'Azur opened up to larger numbers
of visitors than ever before. It was still the preserve
of the wealthy, however. The P.L.M. train line (which
ran the famous *Train Bleu*, or Blue Train, from 1922)
was inaugurated in 1864, as part of the Second
Empire's great scheme to modernize France.

The Scott Château, with
its style-setting diversity of
architecture, overlooks its
magnificent garden.

Children playing on the beach.
Engraving from the *Journal des Demoiselles*, *circa* 1890.

Women on the beach.
Watercolor and lithography, 1895.

Hôtel Metropole — Cannes — A Tennis Match

Until then, the trip from Paris had taken eleven
days in twelve stages, a Herculean journey that no
doubt discouraged many people. The new means of
transport meant that the region could shake off its
reputation as a sort of open-air hospital, and
instead begin to attract aristocrats, wealthy
bourgeois families, and artists, all eager to discover
the delights of the Côte d'Azur. Joseph William
Mallord Turner, John Ruskin, Robert Louis
Stevenson (who stayed at the Villa Bassamo in
Menton during the winters of 1863 and 1864), and
Edward Lear, the master of nonsense verse, all came
to visit the region, attracted by the wonderful
quality of the light and its reputation as an
enchanting holiday spot.

In 1867, another British gentleman, Thomas
Hanbury, built a Palladian style villa at La Mortola,
near Ventimiglia, on the Italian border. Here he
created the first great English garden in the south of
France, which can still be visited today. Local legend
says he found the perfect spot for his home quite by
chance. While out sailing one day he caught a
glimpse of a large patch of land covered in olive and
citrus trees, and saw the ruins of an old château
reflected in the water. He ordered the captain to drop
anchor just offshore, and never left the spot again.

That same year, Lord Thomas Robinson Woolfield
and his gardener, John Taylor, had a stroke of
genius—they decided to buy up large stretches of
land, build on them, and sell the houses to the

people now flocking to the coast. John Taylor
became his former employer's associate, and in 1884
became the first British vice-consul in Cannes. Today
his descendants manage the Côte d'Azur's biggest
chain of property agents, which still bears his name.
Lord Woolfield, for his part, was behind the region's
first bicycle races, and introduced lawn tennis to
France. Like many of his fellow countrymen, he was
a keen sportsman, and at his sumptuous villa, the
Villa Victoria, he laid out the first tennis court on
the continent. (Tennis is undeniably a British
invention, even if there is an ancient French game
along similar lines, called *jeu de paume*.) Lord
Woolfield eventually found himself sitting on a large
fortune. His idea of speculating on the construction
of villas turned out to be a very good one.

But the event that finally set the seal on the
success of the region was in fact entirely fortuitous.
Queen Victoria announced she was to visit the
Riviera. Her visit might almost have seemed out of
place if it had not been caused by a private tragedy.
Her eighth child, Prince Leopold, a hemophiliac,
had died suddenly of a brain hemorrhage while
staying at his villa, the Villa Nevada, in Cannes in
1884, at only thirty years of age. His illness ran in
the family and afflicted another of Victoria's
descendants, Alexis of Russia, son of Czar Nicolas II
and Czarina Alexandra. When Leopold died,
naturally the Queen made a pilgrimage to the town
to grieve for her son. On her return journey, she

The Hotel Regina Excelsior in Nice, one of the first big hotels on the Côte d'Azur and the secondary residence for Queen Victoria. The queen was always very popular in Nice, as she often went shopping there. This passion, shared by her large retinue, was an important source of revenue for Nice shopkeepers.

The entrance hall at the Hotel Regina Excelsior.

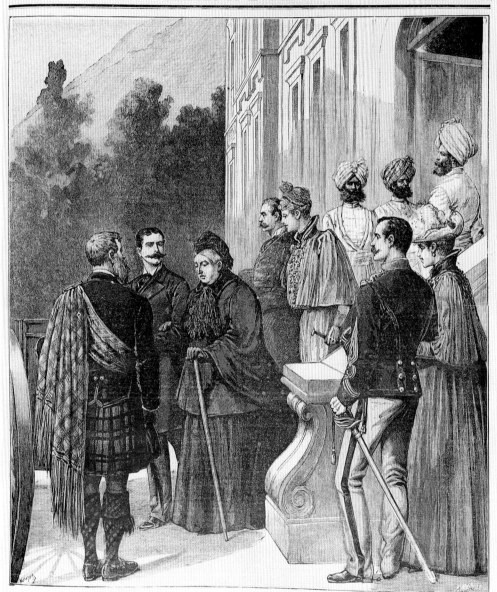

Le Petit Journal

TOUS LES VENDREDIS
Le Supplément illustré
5 Centimes

SUPPLÉMENT ILLUSTRÉ
Huit pages : CINQ centimes

TOUS LES JOURS
Le Petit Journal
5 Centimes

Deuxième Année   SAMEDI 11 AVRIL 1891   Numéro 20

Left:
**Art and fashion on
the Côte d'Azur.**
Old engraving, 1899.
Unlike today, women then wanted to avoid
getting a tan at all costs !

Queen Victoria on the promenade in Grasse.
Le Petit Journal, April 11, 1891.
The queen frequented the Côte d'Azur in
memory of her son, the Duke of Albany,
who had died there. Gradually, the annual
pilgrimage became a genuine pleasure.

Queen Victoria,
out for a ride in Cimiez.

Left :
Queen Victoria.
One of Victoria's whims was to
drive her own donkey carriage.
Jacquot the donkey was soon
famous all along the coast.

The Chalet des Rosiers,
Queen Victoria's
residence in Menton.

871 BEAULIEU. — Hôtel Bristol. — LL.

The Hotel Bristol in Beaulieu was one of the first hotels on the Côte d'Azur, and in those days it was certainly the most modern. It still exists today, but has been divided into luxury apartments.

The Hotel Bristol in Beaulieu, showing the magnificent view over the gulf and the terraced gardens.

discovered Nice, and indicated that she would like to spend some time there. There were no half-measures where Victoria was concerned, and she had an imposing residence built for herself and her retinue, the appropriately named Regina Excelsior. It was situated above the town, on the Cimiez hill, and was a truly gigantic project. Its facade was over two hundred meters long, it contained four hundred bedrooms, two hundred and thirty-three bathrooms, and thirty-three rooms for the staff, with "all modern comforts." It took over four thousand workers a full eighteen months to build. Stephen Liegeard, the author who invented the name Côte d'Azur (Azure Coast) as the title of a book about the region published in 1887, wrote

As a sovereign, she wished to acquaint herself with this colony founded by one of her ministers, and where dwelt the elite of her subjects; as a mother, she wished to pray in the very spot where her son's soul had taken wing...

Victoria came every year from then on, until 1899, two years before her own death. She became a familiar sight to the inhabitants of Nice, as did her impressive suite of Scotch Guards and Bengali officers, chosen because of her particular fondness for their uniforms. The procession must have been quite a sight, particularly as this magnificent and dignified escort used to follow the queen carrying her tea service. It was even decided to install a tram line up the Cimiez hill for the many visitors eager to get a glimpse of her at home. Some were lucky

enough to avoid the excursion by bumping into her in town, where, in between two pleasant coach rides, she loved to shop.

Peaceful Colonization

By the end of the nineteenth century, the Riviera was definitely on its way. Canny businessmen began to develop magnificent palatial hotels for their well-heeled clientele. The well-known furniture maker Maple built the sumptuous Bristol Hotel in Beaulieu. It was inaugurated on January 1st, 1899, and for a while could justly claim to be the most beautiful hotel on the whole of the Mediterranean coast. It had over three hundred rooms and nearly two hundred employees, and a magnificent round dining room opening onto a sea view. It became an absolute reference for upper-class travelers from the drawing rooms of Chelsea and Mayfair, who were just as likely to bump into friends and acquaintances there as at the Savoy back in London. The hotel's success was such that it soon became necessary to build a new wing to accommodate all the servants traveling with their employers.

A number of other, more modest hotels were built after the Bristol, all with evocative names to remind the travelers of their distant homeland: the London House and the Westminster, the Grand Hotel des Anglais in Nice, the Family House in Villefranche, and the Empress Hotel in Beaulieu.

**The Promenade des
Anglais in Nice,** *circa* 1890.
Built on the model of Brighton
Pier, the casino on the pier
has now been destroyed.

Left:
The Villa Éléonore-Louise.
Lord Brougham and
guests at a reception.

The pier and the Nice casino, *circa* 1896.

Opposite page, clockwise:
The Villa Livesey in Beaulieu.
"Florence in the South of France."

A vintage postcard of the Beaulieu Hotel.

The Villa Maryland, built on a cape overlooking the
Mediterranean, and surrounded by cypress trees.

HOTEL BEAU-LIEU

Other businesses soon followed suit, such as Major John Warde's Anglo-French Garage.

The visitors who now came to the region can be classed as the first real tourists. The more well-off among them imitated their aristocratic predecessors and decided to settle there. Signs of their presence were to be seen all around. More and more villas were being built. From Beaulieu to Menton, the whole coastline began to sprout weird and wonderful follies set in fabulous gardens. Although these varied a great deal in style and taste, they followed two main tendencies: a taste for exotica, such as at the Villa Livesey or the magnificent Villa Maryland; and the adherence to the old, familiar way of life, giving a rather odd impression of a sun-bathed little England, with homes bearing such evocative names as Flowerland Cottage, property of the Countess de Roydeville Pringall. Each new tourist smitten with the delights of the Riviera looked for a patch of land where he could settle and leave his mark, and as the population rose, so the new arrivals had to go farther and farther from the main tourist centers to find their piece of heaven.

Gradually some tiny villages became popular, eventually reaching fame and fortune as Cannes had done earlier in the century. The best example of this is the spectacular development of the peninsula of St.-Jean-Cap-Ferrat. It was an arid, barren spit of land without even a spring to water it, just a tiny fishing port where a few families scratched a living.

Its very name speaks of the absolute poverty that reigned there. Saint Jean was a hermit who chose this rocky, deserted headland to retire from the evils of the world; while *ferratus* is the Latin term for wild or desolate. The setting of the promontory jutting out into the sea was magnificent though. Nietzsche had fallen in love with the mystic beauty of the scenery and had expressed his desire to spend the rest of his days here.

And so when in 1876, Désiré Polonnais, the enterprising and far-sighted mayor of Villefranche, decided to construct a reservoir on the cape, the crowds moved in. Baroness Beatrice Ephrussi de Rothschild and King Leopold of Belgium were two of the first to spot the site's potential, bidding millions for the best sites, but, as was by now customary, it was the British who made up most of the visitors. From Cannes to Nice and from Monaco to Menton, they were now the peaceful colonists of a coast they had once tried to conquer with cannons.

A Taste for Exotica

The Villa Livesey was built in 1890 in Beaulieu by a Major Livesey, on a piece of land measuring some twenty-five thousand square meters. It is a mixture of ancient Greek and Florentine Renaissance styles. Today the villa belongs to a property developer who had hoped to divide it into apartments, but who sadly went bankrupt, leaving the villa a shadow of its

Château de l'Anglais, Nice.

Flowerland Cottage, Beaulieu.

former self. However, one can still see traces of the taste for exotica that had already prompted Thomas Hanbury to create the half-Greek, half-medieval style of La Mortola.

In 1904, a British gentleman named Arthur Wilson purchased ten acres of land on the peninsula of St.-Jean-Cap-Ferrat. Here he built a splendid Florentine style villa with some thirty rooms and a magnificent patio framed by two levels of arcades resting on columns of pink marble. Despite its American-sounding name, the Villa Maryland is a fine example of the typically English dream, which considers classical culture and the Renaissance Italy of Raphael and Michelangelo as the absolute pinnacle of civilization. The villa has welcomed several distinguished guests in its time, including King Edward VII, Randolph Churchill, and his promising young son, Winston, who was to be a keen visitor to the south of France all his life. Today, the villa is still intact, but has been divided into three apartments.

The Château de l'Anglais, standing on the edge of Nice, towards Villefranche, was built by Colonel Smith, a retired army officer who had served in India. It is probably the finest example of turn-of-the-century architecture inspired by exotic climes; a nostalgic homage to the sweetness of life on the Bengal river. The traditional rules of architecture are totally ignored, and the building, which dominates the bay, resembles a dream set in stone, with its fluid

lines and improbable curves. It stands directly on the rocky flank of the cliff, the refuge of a man seeking to flee the world. This splendid building shows the extraordinary optimism of the period — the belief that progress makes everything possible, more than the grandest speeches ever could.

The other great tendency of English taste at the beginning of the twentieth century results in the rather curious sight of mansions of the sort one expects to find in Surrey or Kent transplanted to the Mediterranean. All the elements are there, directly imported from Britain — the bow and sash windows, the exposed beams... Just like Michael Scott a few years earlier in Cannes, many settlers now chose to make themselves feel at home by recreating the exact same atmosphere they had known back in England — with a few added comforts, of course. As Somerset Maugham warned, you could be in the middle of a desert and still come across a pair of English women, sitting behind a dune, sipping tea from Wedgwood cups and saucers, sheltered by a parasol...

These are just a few examples of this unusual, even rather eccentric lifestyle, which created a marvelous but utterly artificial culture to suit its needs. For if one characteristic of the Riviera needs to be highlighted above all others, it is that this area is in many ways a totally man-made creation — a fact which is all too often forgotten. To take just one example, vintage photographs of the region show just how sparse and scrubby the vegetation was,

much closer to a Greek landscape than to the luxuriantly watered gardens on the Côte d'Azur today. In those days, trees were few and far between, and the whole stretch of coast resembled a bare lunar landscape. The palm trees that are now such a fundamental part of the image of towns like Cannes, for example, with its famous beach-front avenue, the Croisette, were in fact only planted in 1871.

The story repeats itself along the coast. Different types of trees were brought to the region by train and boat, where they were carefully transplanted and nurtured for their precious shade. Eucalyptus trees were brought from Australia, cypresses from Mexico, agaves from South America, and other rare species were imported from all five continents, blending the earth from their roots with the Mediterranean soil. It was the vision of a few dedicated souls that changed the face of the Riviera so completely, bringing its arid hills a new and luxuriant beauty. Thomas Hanbury at La Mortola set the ball rolling, importing thousands of rare species from all over the world, and acclimatizing a number of tropical varieties. He left a botanical collection which is still unique today. The tropical gardens of Eze and Monaco owe a great deal to his experiments. It was in this way that the Riviera became a veritable garden of Eden, where plants and trees from different continents grow together, just as, in the glittering society occasions that are a regular feature of life on the Côte d'Azur, people from all over the world mingle.

This was the time when the future was conceived of as a vast panorama of progress, where nothing was out of reach, and even the most extravagant of dreams might come true. The Baroness Beatrice Ephrussi de Rothschild, for instance, became known for the stupendous scale of the project she undertook in the garden of her Villa Ile de France in St.-Jean-Cap-Ferrat. She wanted the rocky promontory on which the house stood to look like the prow of an ocean-going liner. To be certain the finished garden would conform to her plans, she did not hesitate to dynamite the hills round about until they were the right shape, and ordered thousands of tons of earth to be dumped on the bare rock to provide a base for her garden. Her exacting nature, allied with her vast wealth, meant she could take the adventure to its limits. She purchased large quantities of antiques which she had delivered to the station in Beaulieu, only then selecting the pieces worthy of figuring in her haven of flowers. Soon, the young baroness was able to revel in the perfection of the dream home she had created for herself. From her windows, she could survey the labors of the bevy of gardeners, who all had to wear a French sailor's uniform, including the traditional beret with its red pompom. For the house itself, the lovely baroness had initially asked the first architect (of fifteen!) to create a house entirely out of painted canvas, a sort of giant tent to be erected *in situ*. This little operation cost her the equivalent of several million of today's

The church of Saint Michael in Beaulieu
was built by local English inhabitants and
consecrated by the Archbishop of York himself.

**The church of Saint
George, Cannes.** Like
many public buildings in
the area, it was paid for by
donations from the local
English community.

The playwright Edmond Rostand and the great actress Sarah Bernhardt.

The *Cercle Nautique* club where the Cannes conferences (and a number of other less serious events) were held. It was one of the real social hotspots of the coast.

euros. She soon tired of it, however, and donated it to the prestigious research institute, the Institut de France, which still owns it today.

The English also brought their own brand of civilization to the region. They funded the construction of a number of public buildings, such as the famous church of Saint Michael in Beaulieu, which was consecrated by the Archbishop of York in person, and where services are still held. Or the church of Saint George in Cannes, which to this day belongs to the Crown of England and is therefore not under the authority of the local diocese. They also carried on funding the improvements to public roads, building for example the three roads that opened up the Cap Martin peninsula for development. Another innovation was the creation of gentlemen's clubs to rival the best in London. To be sure no home comfort was forgotten, they even built a golf course at Mont-Agel, on the hills above Monaco. Every month special boats would deliver lawn turf specially shipped from Britain.

This meeting of two cultures must at times have seemed deeply mysterious and surprising to the local inhabitants, even if the shopkeepers and other local businesses were of course delighted by the arrival of these wealthy new customers. Any number of anecdotes have found their way into local legend, but one of the most enduring is the story of Queen Victoria and the one-legged man. Because of his handicap this native of Marseilles used to travel

around in a little cart pulled by dogs. A regular sight along the coast, he spent the winter begging in the villages round Villefranche and Beaulieu, sometimes venturing as far afield as Nice. Queen Victoria was at this time especially fond of carriage rides along the coast, and eventually she noticed the poor man. As he always greeted her carriage most politely, she got into the habit of asking one of her ladies-in-waiting to give him a few coins. The old man was always most effusive in his thanks, and soon found an original way of expressing his deep gratitude. He had a board fixed on to his cart inscribed with the words "By Special Appointment to Her Majesty the Queen." Word of this quickly got around, and people up and down the coast delighted in the joke. The rumor eventually reached London. The queen didn't know whether to laugh or cry, but in the end requested that the sign be removed, secretly paying the man a sum of money to ensure it was never seen again.

Fashions and Fantasies

The Côte d'Azur was a piece of heaven on earth, where life was leisurely, where time moved at a different rhythm. Cannes was rather conventional, even staid, but Nice and Monte Carlo became a mecca for all sorts of pleasure-seekers. People were spending fortunes in restaurants, and some London tourist guides, like the Grant Richards guide for 1908, were informing visitors to the region that it

The *Cercle Nautique* club.
Lots of yachtsmen dropped anchor here, without ever leaving port! It was here, on March 27th, 1884, that Queen Victoria's son, the Duke of Albany, was struck down with his fatal illness.

The casino in Monte Carlo.
The Schmit Room and its roulette tables.

Evening gowns dating from 1900.
Only the finest outfits were fit to grace a
reception at any one of the many
exclusive clubs on the Côte d'Azur.

The yacht *Aïlsa* belonging to the Walker family. It was famed as one of the loveliest on the Côte d'Azur.

The Hotel Negresco, Nice. Built by a visionary businessman from Romania, Mr. Negresco, and inaugurated in 1912, the Negresco replaced the Bristol as the finest hotel on the coast. Unfortunately, only two years later, the world was to slide into war, destroying the whole way of life on which these grand hotels depended.

was always possible to come to an arrangement with one's waiter (in exchange for a large tip, of course) to transfer part of one's expenditure to the bill of a drunken Russian grand duke (there was one in every hotel). In fact, the Russians soon came to call the French *centimisky*, thanks to their habit of working out bills to the last centime.

It was at this time that the major hotels were founded, many of which rapidly acquired an international reputation for their luxury. Cannes witnessed the opening of the first Cercle Nautique club, founded by the Duke of Vallombrosa, the most Parisian of Spaniards, and a familiar face in all of London's most fashionable haunts. The club quickly became the most chic on the coast. It played host to various members of the immensely wealthy Rothschild family, crowned heads of Europe, and such luminaries as actress Sarah Bernhardt (who often gave a private show for Queen Victoria, one of her most fervent admirers), opera singer Fedor Chaliapin, and the inventors of cinema, the Lumière brothers. In fact, the Lumière brothers, based in Cap d'Ail, made a number of films on the Côte d'Azur, including their very first work to be shown in public, a short film showing a train arriving in the station at La Ciotat.

Life on the coast for such visitors was a whirl of pleasure. There were regattas to attend between regular trips to the theater and gala dinners; the yachts taking part were the most luxurious ever seen.

The Richardson family's *Coelina* had a dining room that could seat ninety guests. It was eventually decided to create a race course overlooking the sea at La Bocca, so that the wealthy clientele of the Riviera could carry on their favorite—and very British— hobby of horse racing here as well as in Deauville.

Other popular spots were the Cercle de la Méditerranée, with its wildly successful dancing matinees, and Rumplemayer's, the fashionable tea rooms that belonged to the same family that owned the legendary Angelina's in Paris. An enterprising Romanian opened a hotel in 1912 on the Promenade des Anglais in Nice, naming it the Negresco, after himself. The new hotel was so magnificent that it even toppled the Bristol from its position as the best hotel on the Riviera. Mr. Negresco had a particular vision for his hotel, and chose the great architect Niermans, known as the Offenbach of architecture, to design the building. The result was rather like a wedding cake, decorated in wreaths and scrolls. The story goes that to celebrate the hotel's opening, Louis Blériot, the first man to fly across the English Channel, had planned to land his aircraft on the roof, before deciding against the idea.

The modern-minded prince of Monaco, Charles III, made the principality the place to be seen. Monte Carlo expanded its casino, and the crowds thronged to the roulette wheels and baccarat tables. The casino first opened in 1863, and in 1879 a

226 MONTE-CARLO la Place du Casino

A vintage postcard of Monte Carlo, showing the casino. Opened in 1862, the casino also has an opera house designed by the legendary Charles Garnier. After a few misadventures, it eventually found success under the direction of the businessman François Blanc, who left a fortune worth some 400 million euros. ("An honest sum," as Baron Rothschild said).

The terrace of the Café de Paris, Monte Carlo.

The Hotel Regina Excelsior, Nice.
The monumental staircase hints
at the luxury of the interior.

The Duc de Vallombrosa's château, Cannes.
Medieval in design, this château is one of the loveliest on
the Côte d'Azur. Despite his Spanish name, the duke was
a familiar face on the Paris party circuit and was the man
behind the celebrated Cannes-La Bocca horse race.

388 MONTE-CARLO. — L'Hôtel de Paris. — LL.

387 MONTE-CARLO. — L'Hôtel de Paris. — LL.

The Hotel de Paris in Monte Carlo. Built to the design
of the grand hotel on the rue Scribe in Paris, it was
inaugurated in 1864. François Blanc, its director, grasped that
the ultimate in luxury brought his well-heeled clients back
again and again.

L'EMPEREUR D'AUTRICHE EN FRANCE

752. - MONTE-CARLO. - Café de Paris

Édition Giletta phot., Nice

Empress Elizabeth of Austria and her husband on the Côte d'Azur. They stayed at Cap Martin, near Empress Eugénie's residence, and the imperial neighbors would occasionally meet and reminisce about the old days.

The Café de Paris, Monte Carlo.

theater was added, designed by Charles Garnier, the architect of the opera house in Paris, which still bears his name. But the real boom in the Riviera's hotel trade was the work of the brilliant and ambitious billionaire François Blanc, director of the recently founded Société des Bains de Mer, today a prestigious hotel chain. He was the first man to have a global vision of this new pleasure-seeking culture. A series of grand hotels opened along the coast, such as the Hermitage in 1906, and the establishment that was to become the famous Hotel de Paris was modernized. The restaurants were full to bursting with city gentlemen on vacation. The directors of these luxury hotels made sure no detail, no matter how small, was neglected, and nearly all the produce was imported—even the fish—so that the clients would feel at home with familiar flavors. Lieutenant-Colonel Newnham Davis, the editor of the Grant Richards guide, liked to tell the story of how he had had to implore one hotel director, Monsieur Fleury, to make him a special meal using local ingredients. This often led to ridiculous situations. At the same hotel, a British visitor was amazed to find superb vintage wines at very cheap prices on the menu. The wine waiter, when questioned, explained the multifaceted phenomenon with a sorrowful air: the wines were too fragile to survive the trip to Paris intact, the people who won at the casino only drank champagne, those who lost could hardly even afford a beer, and as a result, the

cellars were overflowing with excellent bottles that nobody drank!

The hotels of the Côte d'Azur were now the most luxurious in the world. They aroused the curiosity of a great lady, dressed all in black, who came to the Riviera several times in the 1890s. Though accustomed to the ultimate in opulence, she uncharacteristically consented to stay in a hotel without first demanding that it be redecorated to her requirements. She was the Empress Elizabeth of Austria, better known as Sissi, in mourning for her son Rudolph, who died from a gunshot wound near his hunting lodge in Mayerling in 1889, under mysterious circumstances. Now she made the trip more and more frequently, staying at the Grand Hotel in Cap Martin, where she reserved the entire ground floor. Her presence was a great honor for the hotel.

Meanwhile, in a hotel nearby, another sovereign was also suffering great anguish. Eugénie, formerly Empress of France, was living a retired life in the Villa Cyrnos, surrounded by portraits of her only child, killed by Zulus in an ambush in South Africa while fighting in the British army. The heir to the imperial throne had been forced into exile in 1870 after the defeat and abdication of Napoleon III, and had joined the British army. The two women met frequently, and spoke of everything but past sufferings. On occasion, Sissi's husband Franz Joseph would come to visit, and Sissi would arrange to have his mistress, Katherine Schratt, come too, in

The flights of stairs leading to the casino in Monte
Carlo. It is often claimed that the steps were a temptation
for those unlucky gamblers wishing to end it all.

The casino and terraces, Monte Carlo, *circa* 1900.
The business mogul François Blanc ruled his financial
empire from here. The Prince of Wales, the future
Edward VII, is said to have complained:
"At the casino, whether red *or* black, it's always
Blanc ['white' in French] who wins."

Monte Carlo.
General view over Monaco
and the bay. Engraving by
Deray, *circa* 1895.

A poster by Mucha, advertising the delights of Monte Carlo, 1899.

Henry James.

Paul Bourget, Edith Wharton and Joseph Conrad at the Madrague, on the Giens Peninsula, *circa* 1920.

all discretion. While the sovereigns talked, Katherine would be sent off to play at the Monte Carlo casino. (After the death of Franz Joseph, she was completely ruined by her gambling habit.) Sissi, her husband, and his mistress formed a curious trio, but one which seemed to keep all concerned happy enough. Even under the midday sun, Sissi lost none of the habits that had branded her an eccentric all over Europe. She walked for miles along the paths used by the customs service, early in the morning or late at night. She was also fond of walking unannounced into gardens that took her fancy. Most un-royal behavior! One day in Nice, this little foible nearly cost her her life; a certain Madame X (her name has unfortunately been lost in the mists of time) spotted an unfamiliar figure wandering amongst her orange trees, and set her four vicious dogs loose. A keen sportswoman, the empress put on a rare burst of speed to escape the slavering jaws—luckily she was very fit!

Across the Pond

Already, a few Americans were beginning to find their way to this holiday heaven: Henry James, Paris Singer, Ralph Curtiss, and Gordon Bennett, to name just a few. They came to sample the culture and lifestyle of the old Europe, which some of them found more to their taste than others. The French author Valéry Larbaud sketched a humorous portrait of an illustrious American staying at the Majestic in Nice (which opened in 1908):

> *I very much liked this hotel at the center of the world... It is mentioned in the diary of a great nineteenth-century author from abroad. He praises it, but with one reservation: there was no soap to be found in his room. He had just arrived in Europe for the first time, and he did not know that people here are used to choosing their own soap which they bring with them in their suitcases... He thought that nobody in Europe used soap at all.*

It was at this time that Henry James, Edith Wharton's tyrannical master and great friend, visited his old friend Paul Bourget in Costebelle, near Hyères. Both were recognized as great writers, but Paul Bourget had had much more success in financial terms. His property in Costebelle was so splendid that James wrote a self-pitying letter to his brother about it, mildly exhibiting his masochistic tendency, complaining that he would never be able to afford to live in such luxurious and pleasant surroundings. He finally came around to the view that it was better that way, and when he left for Italy he was convinced that such a wealth of comfort would only end up sapping his creative juices. As previously discussed, Edith Wharton's view on this question was diametrically opposed to that of Henry James; all she remembered afterward was his wondering admiration for the region, which he only half-succeeded in disguising.

269. — Beaulieu.
Vapeur américain en rade.

La Côte d'Azur.

An American steamboat
entering the bay at Beaulieu.

The *Lysistrata* in the bay at Villefranche.
This 96-meter-long steamer was one of the
most luxurious of its day. Its owner, the New
York magnate John Gordon Bennett, was a
fixture on the Côte d'Azur at the time.

Gordon Bennett, owner-director of the *New York Herald Tribune*, was without doubt one of the most eccentric and colorful characters of the day. He was mad about yachting (his friends nicknamed him Commodore), and he used to sail the oceans in his sumptuously fitted-out yacht, the *Lysistrata*, which measured nearly three hundred feet in length. Whether they admired or detested him, nobody could remain indifferent. He fell in love with the town of Villefranche, which seemed to him to capture all the purity of ancient Greece, and he dropped anchor there. His arrival was manna from heaven for the local shopkeepers—he ordered astronomical quantities of vegetables, meat, bread, and wine. In return, he demanded that a red carpet be laid out permanently around the port so he would not dirty his shoes. He entertained himself by occasionally choosing an innocent passerby to push into the water unawares, then paying them handsomely for the pleasure afterward. One day, he ordered his staff to scupper a fisherman's boat that had committed the sin of tying up next to his freshly painted yacht. One friend reportedly quipped that Bennett, when sober, he had all the

BEAULIEU-sur-MER. — La Petite Afrique

A view of the part of Beaulieu
known as "Little Africa."

BEAULIEU-sur-MER — Villa Namouna

**Villa Namouna in
Beaulieu** and its
magnificent garden.

worst faults of the Scots, and when drunk, the worst of the Irish.

He was a well-known face in all the grand hotels along the coast. If he thought his lunch was slow to arrive, he would pretend to chew on the carpet while mooing like a cow. On other occasions, if the restaurant was full and could not seat him immediately, he would whip out his checkbook and offer to buy it on the spot. He was generous to a fault, and a great gourmet. He established a rapid road link between Beaulieu to Nice to give better

access to La Réserve, a wonderful new restaurant he had just discovered.

He eventually grew tired of playing with his yacht, and settled on dry land, in a villa in the Petite Afrique district of Beaulieu. This part of town got its name because it was the only place along the coast where bananas would mature. Bennett christened his château Villa Namouna. It was later purchased by François Coty, inventor of the legendary perfume Chanel No. 5 and owner of the *Figaro* newspaper. The property has now been divided into apartments.

Ralph Curtiss was another eccentric billionaire. He built one of the loveliest villas on the Riviera in 1902, Villa Sylvia, named after his wife. It was meant to match his other fabulous residence—a palace in the heart of Venice.

Finally, Paris Singer was another fabulously wealthy American who came to France looking for a good time. His father, the New York sewing machine magnate Isaac Singer, had named him Paris because he was born in the French capital. Because of his generosity, Paris Singer was nicknamed "the socialist billionaire." For example, on May 1st, Labor Day, he invited all the men working on his villa, as well as their families, to a restaurant for lunch. He is most famous for his stormy affair with the dancer Isadora Duncan, with whom he had a child. In fact, Isadora had two children, who died in tragic circumstances—drowning in the Seine after the car they had been left in rolled into the river; the chauffeur had forgotten to put the handbrake on. Paris and Isadora arrived in St. Jean in 1909, and bought up several villas to build what was to become the Château Singer.

The *Belle Époque*

The tourist guides from the early years of the century were full of helpful advice to stop travelers getting into trouble through brazenness or negligence. "We recommend travelers wear light woolens, take an overcoat, and even a muffler, and never stroll in the sun without a parasol." They gave dire warnings about the adverse effects of too much sunlight on the complexion. Yet this was not enough to discourage the hordes of affluent holidaymakers—aristocrats, artists, and intellectuals—who now came to the Riviera to take advantage of its unparalleled opportunities for social success, as well as its mild winters. The *belle époque* was well and truly underway. To miss the season would have been a terrible *faux pas*. The Riviera was now a fixture in the socialite's calendar. Every winter, aristocrats and industrial magnates rubbed shoulders in the restaurants and hotels. Lady Duff Gordon, better known as Lucile, the name she gave her line of lingerie, and who had survived the sinking of the *Titanic*, might meet Monsieur Menier, the chocolate king. Together, they might watch Caroline Otéro pass by on the arm of a Russian prince. (Caroline Otéro spent such a fortune at the Monte Carlo casino that she was completely ruined. In the end, the Société des Bains de Mer allowed her a small pension, in recognition of the money she had spent so freely in their establishments.) Nearby one might have spotted George Bernard Shaw, watching the crowds with a sardonic eye. The whole of human vice was there to be dissected by his rapier wit: here a ladies' man, there a "Sapphic lounge lizard," a bourgeois family, or a high-class prostitute—all rubbing shoulders in polite disdain. The scene would certainly have inspired Oscar Wilde to produce a

The Villa Madrid in Cannes stood in a huge park. It belonged to André Capron, originally from Paris but later Mayor of Cannes. The villa hosted some of the most luxurious parties ever held on the Riviera.

Oscar Wilde, who arrived on the Côte d'Azur in 1898. He stayed at the Grand Hotel des Bains in La Napoule, as a guest of his old friend Frank Harris. Harris, an essayist as well as a wealthy businessman, hoped the stay would reinvigorate Wilde's creative talent.

The Battle of Flowers, Nice. First held in 1877, the event takes place along the grand Promenade des Anglais.

The yachts *Britannia* and *Aïlsa*. The *Britannia*, belonging to the Prince of Wales, sailed back and forth between Cannes and Monte Carlo.

The Villa Kerylos, Beaulieu, was built by Théodore Reinach in the style of a Greek villa from the days of Pericles.

fabulously scathing play, if only he had come to the Riviera a few years earlier. He only came to La Napoule in 1898 as the guest of his old friend Frank Harris, staying at the Grand Hotel des Bains. Frank Harris was a wealthy businessman and essayist in his spare time, and hoped to breathe new life into Wilde's creative spirit. Here, in this Mediterranean atmosphere that he loved so much, Frank believed Oscar would find the will to write again. But his spell in Reading Gaol had done its work, and the wittiest of writers in the English language — banished from polite society, separated from his children — was a broken man. He never wrote again.

It was the age of the grand ball, vaudeville shows, and receptions, at which, as often as not, mistresses would be invited along with wives. In 1896, a journalist from the magazine *La Vie Parisienne* wrote, rather spitefully, that Cannes was a cesspit of debauchery, which "dips its tail in the Mediterranean to restore and renew its ever-changing love affairs." One of the heights of the season in erotic terms was without contest the famous Battle of Flowers, that has taken place on the Promenade des Anglais every year since 1877. A group of genuine maidens — followed by ladies perhaps less pure — throw flowers and handfuls of petals at the crowd of admirers and rivals. Even high society ladies took their place in the parade: for example the famously beautiful Adela Weisweller, widow of a rich Englishman, who later married the mayor of Cannes, André Capron. In her

salon in the Villa Madrid one might meet Alfonso XIII, the young king of Spain, or the kings of Sweden, Norway, Romania, Portugal, as well as high-ranking French politicians. Every Monday she laid on a supper and dance for four hundred people, and for eight to nine hundred on Saturdays. She hosted magnificent dinners *à la française*, where the waiters were dressed in full livery and powdered wigs. Guests came dressed in top hat and tails, a Maharajah's costume, or disguised as the electricity fairy, depending on the theme of the party and their mood. Adela had the garden filled with deer and parrots to amuse her guests, who could spend the night outside, lit by flaming torches, before slipping away in the early hours.

The Riviera was a magnet for all sorts of eccentrics, socialites, and inhabitants of the twilight demi-monde. Take Grand Duke Michael for instance, brother of the Russian Czar Nicolas II, who was more or less condemned to exile in France because he had married beneath his station. He was an extremely keen sportsman and loved all things English. He spent every day at the Mandelieu golf course, and was followed everywhere he went by his two faithful valets. At tea-time, one of them boiled water while the other milked a cow, specially brought along to guarantee the freshness of the product... The grand duke would only use his private train for his many journeys, and hated traveling at speed, as this prevented him from seeing the landscape as he

liked. He therefore forbade his train drivers to go faster than thirty miles per hour which, even in those far distant days, caused considerable disruption and delays to other passengers!

There was also Theodore Reinach, a banker and amateur archaeologist, who spent nearly three hundred million francs on building an exact replica near Beaulieu of the residence of a great Athenian from the time of Pericles, christened the Villa Kerylos. Every detail, even down to the furnishings, had to be historically accurate, and the builders sweated blood trying to accommodate Reinach's demands and still install modern heating and electrical systems. Theodore Reinach was a member of parliament, and demands on his time meant he could only spend three weeks a year in his extravagant holiday home.

But without a shadow of a doubt, the most prominent visitor to the Riviera in these years was the Prince of Wales, to be crowned Edward VII in 1901. He was nearly seventy years old at the time of his coronation, and he had spent all of those years waiting in the wings for his mother, Queen Victoria, to die. His ascension to the throne heralded in a new modern era, with a very different set of values. No wonder he spent so much time on the continent, where he was able to escape all he detested in British society: its hypocrisy and puritanism, as well as the royal reproaches of his mother. Most of the time he was to be found in Paris or in Biarritz, but

he was also a frequent visitor to the Riviera, where he truly felt at home. He divided his time on the coast between Cannes and Monte Carlo; his yacht, the *Britannia*, was often to be seen in one or the other marina. His presence was indispensable at any society event, and he was a real trendsetter— sometimes unconsciously, as when he turned his trousers up when playing golf one rainy day. Straight away, tailors all over Europe began incorporating turn-ups into their trouser patterns. The prince was also something of a gourmand, and he definitely had an eye for the ladies. The two foibles combined gave us the name of a classic dessert still popular in restaurants today. One day in a small restaurant on the Croisette, where today the stars gather during the Cannes Film Festival, he ordered some crepes with orange sauce. They were delicious, and he asked the cook what the dish was called. As it happened, she had not thought to give her creation a name. The prince gallantly dedicated the dish to the charming young lady he was dining with, who went by the name of Suzette. And thus was her name preserved for posterity.

Paradoxically it was these frequent, often indiscreet, escapades that meant the prince was later able to rely on the friendly support of the French people, as none of his ancestors could, when in 1904 he negotiated the Entente Cordiale between England and France. This treaty ended the rather delicate Fachoda episode (two colonial expeditions, one

A still from the 1930 film, *Le Mystère de la Chambre Jaune,* directed by Marcel L'Herbier and shot in the Scott Château.

French and one British, met at Fachoda, on the upper Nile; neither wanted to give way to the other) which had brought the two nations to the brink of war and reversed the military alliances in place at the time. The Entente Cordiale paved the way for warmer relations between London and Paris in opposition, and put an end to centuries of political and military rivalry, and was soon—and tragically—called into action against the ambitions of Kaiser Wilhelm II.

The End of an Era

Towards the end of the nineteenth century, the Riviera was a constant whirl of pleasure, and it naturally drew the most daring artists and creative thinkers. Although Henri Matisse only discovered the delights of Nice in 1917, as early as 1908 the theater in Monte Carlo welcomed the fabulous Russian Ballet and its director Diaghilev, who together were to revolutionize several centuries of dance tradition. Stars like Nijinski and Mikhail Fokine never shone as brightly as they did here under the Mediterranean sun. They were followed by other well-known names like Stravinsky and Leon Bakst, come to share their far-sighted, cataclysmic artistic visions with the world.

Indeed, life on the Riviera at this time can be compared to dancing on the flanks of a volcano. The Côte d'Azur was witnessing the last convulsions of a civilization that was soon to come crashing down. Many of the brightest flames on the Riviera were to be brutally snuffed out by war and revolution. Under the veneer of glitz, there were some terrible stories of human suffering. Take the example of the Russian Princess Souvaroff, who one day decided to rent a magnificent residence to throw an unforgettable party. Her fortune was so immense that she had no real idea of what she was worth.

The Villa Alexandra, Cannes was built by
Eugène Tripet, the French consul in Saint
Petersburg, and named after his wife, a young
Russian aristocrat. The author Prosper Mérimée was
a guest at the inaugural celebrations in 1850.

A few years later, in 1917, she returned to the Riviera totally ruined. She had barely escaped the Russian Revolution with her life. She went to her usual hotel and very humbly asked for a job as a chambermaid. The porter was skeptical, but the princess insisted—she was now penniless, and needed to work to survive. The porter asked what had happened to her palace. She replied that the Bolsheviks had seized it, along with everything else she owned. The porter said he meant her palace just down the road. As it turned out, years before, the night of her party, she had bought the villa on the spur of the moment, signing the deeds between two glasses of champagne, and forgetting the impulse as quickly as it had come. From then on, the princess lived in the villa, a relic of her former extravagance, and ran it as a very exclusive and much sought-after guesthouse.

An even more dramatic story, which also sheds light on life on the Riviera at the time, starts in 1906. The legendary Mata Hari came to the Monte Carlo Opera House to dance in a production of Massenet's *Le Roi de Lahore*. The show was an absolute triumph, as it had been in Paris. As she danced, Mata Hari gradually divested herself of all of her veils (with "graceful gestures that were at once daring yet chaste," as the critics reported). The public was captivated by the magnificent diva; they had never seen anything like it. The colorful crowd of princes and millionaires rushed backstage to try and find Mata Hari's dressing room. Among the adoring fans was one especially enthusiastic Italian gentleman, bowled over by the dancer, throwing handfuls of flowers onto the stage. His name was Giacomo Puccini.

Mata Hari had the world at her feet. She was the queen of scandal, rejecting the morals of the day by flaunting her sexual freedom. Europe was a wonderful place to be, and life in Monaco was the best there was. It was a time when people engage in all kinds of provocative behavior, when they dared to transgress the rules and test the limits of polite society. And yet... on the horizon, storm clouds were gathering. France and Germany were quarreling over military control of the Moroccan port of Agadir. Was it destiny that Mata Hari met a handsome young German officer, Alfred Kiepert, during her stay in Monaco? He fell madly in love with her—a passion that was to prove fatal to her. The dancer moved to Berlin, and followed her rich young lover everywhere, but people believed that she had declared her colors even before the war began. Mata Hari returned to Monaco in 1910 to dance *Antar*, an Oriental ballet to the music of Rimsky-Korsakov. She was overcome with emotion on returning to the scene of her greatest triumph. The eternal traveler, she finally decided to settle down here, in the warmth of the sun, and had a house built on Cap d'Ail. But her plans were overtaken by events, and she never got the chance to enjoy her new home. The Villa Primavera, based on a Roman palace, was eventually finished in the 1920s, three years after its owner had been executed by firing squad for spying.

During the *belle époque*, all paths led to the Côte d'Azur. All of human nature was there—kindness and cruelty, great generosity, tremendous passions, love, and madness. It beckoned to Edith Wharton to come and discover her spiritual home.

"Winter in Cannes".
Advertising poster, 1909.

The Smith Château, Nice, is a splendid example
of the villas one sees dotted along the Cote d'Azur.

Opposite:
A train company poster vaunting
the delights of the Côte d'Azur.

the gods arrive
(1919-1930)

Upon arriving in Hyères, Edith Wharton settled into the Hotel du Parc. From her room she could see the magnificent convent that had formerly been home to a community of nuns from the order of Ste. Claire, which dominated the town from its position high on the hill. Edith, seduced by the building's pure lines and superb sea views, quickly decided that this was where she wanted to live. The site seemed predestined to receive her, located as it was a mere stone's throw from the Villa du Plantier, where the voice of her mentor, the "hermit of Lamb House," Henry James, still seemed to echo in the corridors. The villa was the property of Edith and Henry's mutual friend, Paul Bourget.

Like Edith, the Riviera was having a hard time adjusting to the post-war world. The fortunes of many of the region's foremost families had been swallowed up in the conflict, and nobody yet knew that a new wave of visitors, with very different ideas from their predecessors, was about to hit the Riviera. The summer season, launched by the Americans, was just around the corner, and was to attract hordes of well-heeled and well-connected young people who would shake up the rather staid old guard of pre-war tourists. The Riviera was going to change from a genteel resort where the upper classes took health cures and socialized, to a much racier place, where Europe and America's golden youth lived life to the limits in an attempt to banish the specter of a new world war. And so Edith

Wharton found herself caught between these two worlds; the past that she wished to flee but that gave her sustenance, and the present, which she was not sure she preferred but which gave her the liberty she craved. Paradoxically, it is probably this very contradiction which allowed her to find her niche. She adored her dual nationality: being half-French and half-American she had the best of both worlds, at once at home and a foreigner.

Between Two Worlds

It has often been said that the First World War signaled the end of the old order, a whole civilization—the world of the nineteenth century. For the first time, Europe became aware of her mortality, and this had a profound and long-lasting effect on the social and political realities of the whole continent. Three empires collapsed, and London and Paris went into a long and slow economic decline. The rising stars were now the great cities of North America: New York, Chicago, Philadelphia. The traditionally aristocratic clientele of the Riviera, facing financial ruin or too deeply traumatized by war, melted away like snow. Even the palaces they had built to their glory had suffered in the war. Before 1914, an elegant, colorful, and mixed crowd had thronged to them; after the war, their corridors echoed with the sound of human suffering. Most of them had been transformed into

military hospitals, and the only aristocrats who stayed there during the war years were volunteer nurses, wearing white coats instead of mink, and stethoscopes instead of ropes of pearls. Edith Wharton was living in Paris during this period, and contributed to the war effort by greatly assisting refugees from those areas of France and Belgium invaded by the enemy, making donations to various charities and by running dispensaries. She was made a member of the Legion of Honour, a great honor in France, in recognition of her contribution.

The Americans swept in to blow away the cobwebs from the old Riviera. The bright young things who had grown up on the American east coast were still fascinated by Europe, but now they went to London or Paris rather than Italy. This new generation was separated from their parents by the devastation of the war. Most of the visitors were short of money but were nonetheless determined to live the good life, and try to forget the horrors of the conflict that continued to haunt them. These two factors led them to adopt the Riviera as their own, launching for the first time the idea of the summer season. The coastline was still unspoiled, the waters of the Mediterranean were crystal clear, and all in all the Côte d'Azur seemed a million miles away from the traumas and the deprivation that the rest of Europe was still enduring. Another factor was that it was possible to rent the grand aristocratic residences very cheaply, as they were generally shut for the summer.

The reasons that led Edith Wharton to come and settle on the Riviera, however, were rather different. They are often left to one side, although they provide a key to part of the author's personality and to some of her deepest secrets. She was enchanted by what she saw in the village of Hyères. She felt as if she had been reincarnated "in some warm peaceful temperate heaven of the Greeks, chock-full of asphodel and amaranth." She found herself confronted by "views of land and sea as they never were before, because no previous eyes ever saw them," and noted her first impressions for posterity some years later. She suddenly felt a profound need to come and live in this spot, quite simply she felt as if her future depended on it, as she wrote to her friend Royal Tyler in 1919. She compared the Riviera to Dante's "*cielo della quieta*" that lay beyond the seventh heaven.

In Hyères she felt a magical, magnetic quality, that neither London nor Paris, nor any American city could ever hold for her. This little town on the coast, overlooking the sparkling blue sea, reminded her of the happiest moments of her childhood, when she spent six years criss-crossing Europe with her family. Despite being American through and through, despite having described New York and its high society circles better than anyone before—or since—she had never forgotten her intense pleasure upon discovering the Italian countryside and the palaces of Rome with her father. She became

convinced that it was in the sunshine of the Mediterranean that she would find the strength to rebuild her life.

Now aged fifty-seven, Edith needed to put down new roots to recover the stability that had been sorely lacking in her life of late. She had been divorced from her husband Teddy for six years now, after nearly thirty years of marriage, and was still getting over a significant three-year love affair with the brilliant dandy and womanizer, Morton Fullerton, in which, for the first time, she had known sexual passion. After a few months of intense happiness, their relationship slowly went downhill. She soon recovered from the affair, however, and remained good friends with Fullerton, perhaps because she was grateful to him for having awakened her sensuality and her imagination. Now at the height of her maturity and creative powers, she relied more than ever on finding a balance between the social whirl of life on the Riviera and the quiet and solitude indispensable to her writing (*The Age of Innocence* was published in 1920). She was sure that the Côte d'Azur would provide her with both the moral and physical distance and the time she needed for her writing. However, this does not really explain why she fell in love with the region at first sight, a feeling that was almost irrational in its intensity—particularly as she had a lifetime's experience in controlling her emotions.

She had always loved the sea, and constantly refers to it in her books and in her private correspondence. She wrote of "plunging into" pleasure, being "submerged" by emotion, and "crossing to the other shore." Of course, these are common expressions, but they turn up with such

astonishing regularity in her writings that they surely indicate a pattern of thought. The constantly changing sea, perpetually moving but ever the same, terrifyingly irrational, drew her like a twin soul. The Côte d'Azur echoed her inner voice and a whole range of secret sensations and emotions, without which her life was empty. It was here, in Cannes, that her beloved father, George Frederic Jones, had come to die in 1882. She had already spent many long weeks wandering the paths through the hills, the scent of wild thyme and rosemary on the breeze, with *The Stones of Venice,* a volume by Ruskin, in her hand, seeking to incarnate the emotions he so perfectly described.

The place chosen by Edith Wharton to be her new home was also particularly significant. Was the decision to live in a former convent a sign that she was tired of her society persona, elegant to the tips of her fingers? Her purchase of the old Ste. Claire convent is typical of her hidden duality. Behind her brilliant, seductive facade was a need for an austere solitude. This was not the least of the paradoxes that made Edith Wharton such a fascinating character. Had she not herself concluded, without a hint of bitterness, that for reasons beyond the wit of man, the creative spirit is more fruitful when it is starved? Without an understanding of this side of her personality, there can be no comprehension of the ties that bound her so firmly to her mentor Henry James. Master and pupil were two sides of the same coin, two anxious souls perpetually seeking reassurance. Although they had chosen to follow very different paths, they were both in perfect harmony with their own selves. Henry James was content with his retiring, frugal lifestyle, which

Opposite left:
The Hotel des Anglais and the *Cercle de la Méditerranée* in Cannes, with a view of the casino.

Sam Wooding and his famous band. Jazz was all the rage on the Riviera.

The artist Francis Picabia and the singer Marthe Chenal enjoying a stay on the Riviera.

echoed his open disdain for all things material. Edith's lifestyle seemed to be the complete opposite, but in fact she was following the same path of total commitment to the demands of her art. To differing extents, both writers were dominated by their imagination.

Edith's many homes—in Lenox, Massachusetts, in St. Brice-sous-Forêt near Paris, or here in the south of France—were not simply the extravagances of a wealthy woman of the world, but really played the role of a protective shell. They can be seen as substitutes for the body, for a physicality which she so often denied, but which she nevertheless needed, both to protect her against the world and to allow her to face up to it. The author of works with titles like *Atrophy* and *Disintegration* decided not to bear children to avoid passing on the suffering of being. She went even further in a letter to her friend Sara Norton, comparing the birth of a child to an operation to remove an organ. The convent's former occupants were even more symbolic of her life: the "Clarisses," the Poor Claires, dedicated their lives to God in remembrance of Ste. Claire, companion saint of Francis of Assisi, who herself preached poverty and abnegation. All these echoes of Edith's own life are certainly more than just coincidence. Her writings were inscribed in the very stones of her new home, and, more than for many other writers, Edith's writing was her life.

The Gatsby Years

As the winter season gave way to summer, so one era passed and a new one began. Flappers and playboys from the United States began to spend their summers in the region around Cannes, in Cap d'Antibes and Juan-les-Pins, instantly turning them into the most desirable of holiday locations. The first American visitors brought a fresh, youthful culture with them, that included jazz bands and daring dances, and opened the way for some of the richest men and women in the United States to come and taste the delights of this "Azure Coast", spending their money like water to make sure that this bit of heaven was exactly to their taste. Life on the Riviera became unrecognizable to anyone who had not visited since before the war. It was no longer a resort where people came for their health and to mingle with their aristocratic peers; now it was wild, unbridled, full of bright young things conscience of life's fragility and draining the cup to the dregs before it was too late.

In July 1922 the composer Cole Porter rented an abandoned villa near Antibes. He arrived at the Château de la Garoupe with a gaggle of artist friends, and they were soon joined by a magic circle of wealthy and talented east coast Americans. Cole Porter had chosen to come to the Riviera for the beauty of the scenery of course, but also for more prosaic pecuniary reasons. The elegant crowds who

Zelda and F. Scott Fitzgerald.
The legendary couple who lit up the
Côte d'Azur before their love story
ended tragically with Zelda's madness.

had made the Côte d'Azur the place to be disappeared with the first rays of the April sun, and their fabulous villas were generally available for rent at ridiculously low prices. It was unthinkable for a European aristocrat to remain on the Riviera out of season—they all returned home for a short while before the whole crowd met up again in the highly elegant seaside town of Deauville, on the Normandy coast, for the start of the horse-racing season. The Americans, however, were immune to the fear both of this social *faux pas* and of the summer sun.

The locals must have thought the new arrivals totally dissolute. That first summer saw the arrival of a couple who, although they were by no means famous, were to play a key role in the future of the Riviera and the glory of what was soon, and tragically, to become known as the "lost generation." Gerald and Sarah Murphy were an attractive, young, and wealthy American couple. They had been a fixture of New York high society since the war, and were friends with John Dos Passos, author of the classic *Manhattan Transfer*, and other luminaries of the cultural scene who gathered in the smoky salons of New York's Algonquin Hotel. The Murphys then undertook a tour of Europe, as Edith Wharton herself had done many years before. They were drawn into the magic of 1920s Paris, especially Montparnasse, where they made friends with the circle of artists who frequented the legendary brasseries, the Dôme, the Select, and the Coupole:

Picasso, Braque, Léger, Picabia, Duchamp. The Murphys then traveled south to join their host Cole Porter, and the couple was immediately seduced by the quality of light and the beauty of the views.

It was the Murphys who really launched the Riviera as a summer holiday spot, returning year after year, and bringing with them hordes of celebrities from both Europe and America. Who knows, if the Murphys had not accepted Cole Porter's invitation, the Riviera might never have experienced its second, summer golden age. They persuaded the owner of the Hotel du Cap not to close the establishment entirely over the summer, and then rented a wing to receive their visitors in style. One of their first guests was Gertrude Stein, the renowned American authoress. Little by little, the Murphys gathered around them a glittering circle of brilliant creative minds: Ernest Hemingway, Anita Loos, Calvin Tomkin, Rudolph Valentino, Henry Miller, Alice B. Toklas, and Dorothy Parker, among others. In 1924, just as the Murphys were getting ready to move into their new home—the Villa America—another couple arrived on the Riviera, the legendary, magnificent, but tragic Scott and Zelda Fitzgerald. The pair had come to the Côte d'Azur on the advice of Gertrude Stein, who had assured them that there they would be able to get by on almost nothing.

Astonishingly, one of Scott Fitzgerald's reasons for coming to the Riviera was the fact that Edith

The Grand Hotel des Iles d'Or in Hyères.

F. Scott Fitzgerald at the wheel of his new
Renault 6 CV, with his wife Zelda and their daughter
Scottie.

A still from *The Great Gatsby,* based on
F. Scott Fitzgerald's most famous novel.

Wharton lived there. He was a tremendous admirer
of hers, a fact of which she was at the time unaware.
In 1922 he had written the dialog for a film version
of one of her novellas, *False Dawn,* which had
opened to glowing reviews. The two authors indeed
had a number of points in common—both of them
examined their world of wealthy socialites under the
microscope and found it defective, and both
denounced its overweening vanity. Scott and Zelda
came to live at the Grand Hotel des Iles d'Or in
Hyères in the secret hope of meeting the new owner
of the Ste. Claire convent on the hill. Scott had
brought a manuscript with him that he wanted to
show Edith. He promised himself he would finish
working on it before the summer was out. He was
still looking for a title, but soon settled on one that
suited the text perfectly, *The Great Gatsby.*
Unfortunately, the couple was unable to meet Edith
Wharton on this occasion, as she had already
returned to St. Brice. Fitzgerald eventually sent her a
copy of the published book. Edith, replying by letter,
said she was "touched" by the gesture, "for I feel that
to your generation, which has taken such a flying
leap into the future, I must represent the literary
equivalent of tufted furniture and gas chandeliers."
It was only the next year that the two authors met
finally in Paris. Edith's beloved cousin Walter Berry
was behind the meeting.

In the meantime, Scott and Zelda made the best
of their summer in Hyères, enjoying the sun and the
lively parties. In fact, the couple rapidly became
central to the new American set taking shape. They
were invited to stay at the Hotel du Cap with Gerald
and Sarah Murphy, and at first seemed to take things
easier under this new influence. In *Tender Is the
Night,* Scott Fitzgerald gives a glimpse of the serene
atmosphere of the Hotel du Cap:

> *On the pleasant shore of the French Riviera, about
> halfway between Marseilles and the Italian border,
> stands a large, proud, rose-colored hotel. Deferential
> palms cool its flushed facade, and before it stretches a
> short dazzling beach. Lately it has become a summer
> resort of notable and fashionable people; a decade
> ago it was almost deserted after its English clientele
> went north in April. Now, many bungalows cluster
> near it, but when this story begins only the cupolas of
> a dozen old villas rotted like water lilies among the
> massed pines between Gausse's Hotel des Etrangers
> and Cannes, five miles away.*

The two couples were immediately and
mysteriously drawn to one another. The Murphys
were a solid, united, peaceful couple, while the
Fitzgeralds burned with destructive passion for each
other. Gerald Murphy considered the new friends to
be charming but immature children, and looked on
them with an almost fatherly eye. Scott felt the need
to test this friendship, and was constantly pushing
the limits, seeing how far he could go without
destroying the relationship. He would undress in the
lobby of respectable hotels, paint obscenities on the

walls of luxurious villas, and generally provoke all
sorts of scandals. Meanwhile, Zelda was sinking
deeper into alcoholism—gin was her favorite
drink—and flirting shamelessly. Scott would ignore
this behavior for a while before suddenly exploding
in anger. The Fitzgeralds would regularly dance all
night long, drinking more than was reasonable, and
on occasion even coming to blows. Scott would
drive his new Renault 6CV at high speed along the
narrow, winding country roads as if he were trying
to provoke the accident that would end it all. This
non-stop defiance of the limits of sensible behavior
brought the couple to the brink of tragedy a number
of times. One story goes that early one morning,
after a particularly raucous night, Zelda and Scott
were found comatose in their car, which was slewed
across a railway line. Their rescuers just had time to
save them before the express from Paris roared past.

The Fitzgeralds were the biggest losers at these
games of theirs—by testing their love to the limits,
they destroyed it and each other. They wanted to
bring down the barriers of society; all they
succeeded in doing was harnessing their madness
for a while, channeling it into their work and
convincing themselves that this destructive streak
was a necessary part of their creative enterprise.
Rather than fleeing the place that made it so easy
for them to give free rein to their self-destructive
tendencies, Scott and Zelda grew very attached to
the Riviera. Two years later, *The Great Gatsby* was a

commercial and critical success, allowing the couple
to settle near the Murphys, in the Villa Saint Louis
(today the Hotel Belles Rives) between Juan-les-Pins
and Cap d'Antibes, where they stayed until 1929. It
was here that Ernest Hemingway, himself living
through the first of many marital crises, witnessed a
series of angry scenes between Scott and Zelda.
Hemingway was staying at the Villa America with his
wife and his mistress, and was hypnotized by the
sheer aggressiveness of the couple. He was horrified
by this ritual of mutual destruction, which probably
goes some way to explaining why his judgement of
Scott Fitzgerald's work was so harsh. The Riviera
inspired a curious mixture of feelings in Ernest
Hemingway, a blend of carnal desire, regret, guilt,
and exhilaration, that give a special flavor to his last
book, *The Garden of Eden*, which is set on one of the
beaches he used to visit, right by the Villa Fiamma,
once briefly home to Dorothy Parker and her
"vicious circle" of friends.

It must be said that, despite the often
unpleasantly incestuous nature of such expatriate
circles, the Riviera in those years was a magical,
bewitching place to be, a peaceful haven far from the
madding crowds. Scott Fitzgerald wrote naively to
one of his friends, "Nobody was in Antibes that
summer... except me, Zelda, the Valentinos, the
Murphys, Mistinguet, Rex Ingram, Dos Passos, Alice
Terry, the MacLeishes, Charlie Brackett, Mause Kahn,
Lester Murphy, Marguerite Namara, E. Oppenheimer,

The Hotel Carlton and bathing huts on the Croisette, Cannes, circa 1920. The architect was Charles Dalmas.

The casino in Cannes.

Un Nouveau Palace à Cannes

LE CARLTON HOTEL

M. H. Ruhl, le distingué Directeur et fondateur du Casino Municipal de Cannes, dont l'activité extraordinaire s'emploie, en outre, à l'administration de maintes affaires Hôtelières d'une très grosse importance, vient de doter Cannes d'un Palace magnifique, situé en plein Boulevard de la Croisette, dominant de ses sept étages, le panorama le plus merveilleux qu'il soit possible d'évoquer.

C'est une féerie véritable que de voir ouvert, ordonné, magnifiquement organisé jusqu'en ses moindres détails, prêt à fonctionner, en un mot, cet Hôtel de 250 chambres, développant ses 150 mètres de façades sur le terrain où, il y a huit mois à peine, rien n'existait encore de ce qui est devenu le *Carlton Hôtel* !

Et devant ce prodige de rapidité de sûre organisation, on reste confondu, ne sachant ce qu'il faut le plus admirer, de l'esprit qui a conçue et menée à bien cette remarquable entreprise ou de l'art véritable, de l'élégance et du goût qui ont présidé à la construction à l'aménagement et à l'ameublement somptueux de ce moderne Palace.

Je ne m'étendrai pas sur l'aspect gracieusement élégant des façades. L'ensemble est d'un gout parfait, d'une heureuse harmonie et l'on sent, aux détails architecturaux, tel ce raffinement qui prévoit à chaque fenêtre le sourire d'une corbeille fleurie, qu'un véritable artiste a présidé à l'élaboration des plans du *Carlton*.

Cette impression demeure, sitôt que l'on a pénétré dans le Grand Hall aux multiples pilliers, tout blanc, rehaussé de l'éclat doré des appliques d'éclairage, de la luisance des marbres et du chaud coloris de merveilleux tapis. Sur ce Hall s'ouvrent, à droite le Restaurant précédé d'une superbe terrasse sur laquelle il sera exquis de déjeuner sous la caresse du soleil, ou de paresser délicieusement ; à gauche, un vaste salon de lecture, luxueusement meublé et aménagé. Au fond, enfin, les différents services de la réception ; le majestueux bureau du con-

M. RUHL, *Administrateur-Directeur*

cierge ; les vestiaires, salons de coiffure, billard, bar, ascenseurs, etc., etc.

VUE DU CARLTON HOTEL (Promenade de la Croisette)

Chacun des sept étages de l'Hôtel contient une quarantaine d'appartements, dont les fenêtres s'ouvrent sur l'admirable vision du golfe de Cannes, dans sa plus grande étendue.

Chaque chambre est flanquée d'une salle de bains w.-c., installée avec tous les raffinements du plus moderne confort.

Les chambres elles-mêmes et les salons qui s'y rattachent sont meublés, il est superflu de l'indiquer, avec un luxe et un souci d'élégance parfaits.

Tout, enfin, est minutieusement organisé pour prodiguer aux hôtes du Carlton Hôtel, l'hospitalité la plus fastueuse, la plus intelligemment raffinée et la plus confortable.

Aux mille détails de cette hospitalité, présidera l'homme le plus aimablement distingué qui soit, M. E. Martinez, qui dirige déjà, pendant la saison d'Eté, le Grand Hôtel de Cabourg, dirigera également le Carlton de Cannes et c'est là, pour les hôtes de cette maison, la certitude d'une affabilité élégante et discrète qui ne laissera à leurs plus subtiles exigences, que le temps de se formuler.

A peine ouvert, d'ailleurs, le Carlton Hôtel se verra en grande partie occupé. De nombreux hivernants ont en effet, retenu déjà leurs appartements. Citons parmi eux :

Sir Edmond Sassoon et suite, de Londres ;
Earl & Lady Kinnull ;
M. Eger et famille, de St-Pétersbourg ;
Mlle H. Ritter ;
Mr & Mrs T. Powers, de New-York ;
M. Z. Gubbay et famille, et M. E. Gubbay ;
G. Kentish and party, de Londres ;
M. le Duc de Luynes, Paris,
etc., etc.

Il est des plus heureux, pour notre ville, que l'initiative de M. H. Ruhl s'exerce en sa faveur, si fréquemment, si intelligemment, et nous serons les interprètes de tous ceux qui ont à cœur la prospérité de Cannes, en assurant M. Ruhl, qu'il a bien mérité de la reconnaissance des habitants et des hôtes de la *Perle de la Riviera*.

A. M.

A newspaper article reporting the opening of the Hotel Carlton in Cannes.

La table de M. Bermont, conseiller général des Alpes-Maritimes

L'INAUGURATION DU MIRAMAR

Le " Miramar ", qui dresse sur la Croisette sa massive silhouette de Palace somptueux et international, vient d'ouvrir ses immenses salons par un gala auquel assista le Tout-Cannes élégant.

Dans ce cadre aux vastes proportions vinrent dîner, le premier soir, Altesses couronnées, princes et toutes les personnalités les plus en vue du monde de l'Art et de la Finance.

Une vue d'ensemble du dîner de gala

Photo Novaro

La table du baron de Meyronnet de Saint-Marc

The inauguration of the Hotel Miramar.

The pyjama style
was a great hit on the
Côte d'Azur in the 1930s.

The famous billionaire Frank Jay Gould was the man behind the resorts at Cap d'Antibes and Juan-les-Pins.

The pyjama style, as worn in Juan-les-Pins in the 1930s.

Mannes the violinist, Floyd Dell, Max and Crystal Eastman... Just the right place to rough it, an escape from the world..." He could not have suspected that the very fact that such a select list should choose this spot for their holidays would soon bring in the crowds he sought so strenuously to avoid. Soon, he and his friends would be complaining about the "hordes of tourists" invading their beaches. We can smile about their panic today, as we can smile at the novelist Colette's description of tailbacks of Bugattis and Hispano-Suizas "invading" St. Tropez. For in spite of themselves, the bohemian and artistic elite launched a new fashion for suntans and sea bathing, and a new sense of pleasure in the human body, no longer restricted by corsets and stiff collars. In fact, it was shortly after this that the first nudist area was opened, just down the coast near Toulon. Gradually the restrained British style and elegance that had launched the Riviera was giving way to an American way of life.

The Last Nabobs

The unexpected popularity of the Riviera with the cream of American society was a boon for many hoteliers, saving them from bankruptcy. The owner of the Carlton was not so lucky, however, and had to sell off his hotel cheap in 1919. Major property developers even took it as a cue to build a new wave of luxury hotels. Nice began work to modernize the

Promenade des Anglais, and Cannes built a new casino. The story of this new casino gives a good idea of how times had changed since the beginning of the century.

In 1919 two men, Eugène Cornuché and François André, were hired to run the casino. Although today he is totally forgotten, Eugène Cornuché was a man of exceptional qualities. Physically, he looked tough and uncompromising, but he was in fact possessed of great humanity. He required a lot of his staff, but gave just as much himself as he demanded from others. Eugène Cornuché had started out with nothing, and succeeded by dint of sheer hard work and willpower. Arriving in Paris as a young man along with a friend by the name of Chauveau, with fifteen francs between the two of them, they managed to find work in a hotel, and from this first step worked their way up to become directors of the legendary Maxim's, founded by Maxime Gaillard in 1883. Cornuché turned out to have a natural flair for dealing with people, and brought the cream of Paris society to Maxim's. He was also behind the casino in the summer resort of Deauville. The fact that Eugène Cornuché was now aware of the possibilities offered by the Riviera was proof indeed that a boom was just around the corner. He had a special talent for spotting trends before they got truly underway, and would arrive to pluck the fruit just as it was perfectly ripe. He had a fail-safe method of guaranteeing the success of his undertakings, which

Art - Goût - Beauté

Fashion on the Côte d'Azur. Illustration
from a contemporary fashion revue.

Art - Goût - Beauté

Yachting fashion.

Dressing for tennis.
Designs by Jean Patou, 1925.

Le Costume de bain d'Hermès

HERMÈS
SELLIER
24, Faubourg St-Honoré
PARIS

Hermès advertising its new beachwear line.

Fashion on the Côte d'Azur.
Under the influence of new designers such as
Paul Poiret and Coco Chanel, women were
throwing off their corsets, bobbing their hair,
and sunbathing for the first time.

Advertising brochure for the Wagons-Lits train
company. In the 1930s, thousands of British
holidaymakers travelled to the Côte d'Azur on the
Blue Train, popularly known as the "Magic Carpet."

Renée at the Palm Beach, Cannes, 1931. Photograph by J.-H. Lartigue.

"THE LONGEST GANGPLANK IN THE WORLD"

Weekly Express Service between New York, London and Paris

French Line

Compagnie Générale Transatlantique
New York - Paris

The French Line transatlantic steamer company; offering crossings from New York to Paris.

The *France* leaving New York.

The Palm Beach Hotel pool, Cannes.
Photograph by J.-H. Lartigue.

Breakfast in Monte Carlo.
A room in the Hotel Beau Rivage.
Photograph by J.-H. Lartigue, 1921.

Games on the beach at Cannes.
Photograph by J.-H. Lartigue, 1929.

An automobile race in Monaco.
Photograph by J.-H. Lartigue, 1935.

Juan-les-Pins. This rather neglected resort suddenly came into fashion in 1930.

Juan-Les-Pins. A view of the villas and the casino.

The Provençal. This Antibes hotel was very much in fashion.

Evening gown by Paul Poiret, summer 1929. The gown is in jade and gold lamé with a train attached to the ankle. The corsage is in pink-beige muslin.

Stills from *The Four Horsemen of the Apocalypse*, directed by Rex Ingram.

had already proved its worth in Deauville. He would invite a few select and influential guests for an all-expenses-paid holiday, and then let them spread the word for him. In no time at all, the restaurant attached to the casino, Les Ambassadeurs, was a favorite meeting place for the social elite from all the European capitals. The older generations were curious to see how the place had changed since they were young, but it was really the younger generations who set the ball rolling. Having spent a free holiday on the Riviera, they were hooked, and returned again and again—as paying guests. All over the coast, new hotels sprouted like mushrooms to accommodate these bright young things. Cannes saw the opening of three Art Deco marvels: the Majestic, the Miramar, and the Martinez (seven floors, six hundred rooms). At St.-Jean-Cap-Ferrat, the Grand Hotel was entirely renovated, and in Nice the most luxurious hotel in the world, the Palais de la Méditerranée, was inaugurated.

This last project was the brainchild of a man who was really the grand seigneur of the Côte d'Azur, the American railway billionaire Frank Jay Gould. It was he who launched the resort of Juan-les-Pins. There had been a holiday trade of sorts there since 1882, but the spot did not have a very good reputation. The land was once a swamp. A book published in 1932 describes Juan-les-Pins before Frank Jay Gould took an interest in the site, "Until recently, the walker would find nothing but pine trees in Juan-les-Pins, which to us seems most extraordinary. There were a few mediocre villas scattered as if lost beneath the quivering tops of trees rooted in sea sand... It was a resort with no future." The visionary Mr. Gould devised a plan to improve the beaches, and built a casino and hotel—the Provençal, a palace with two hundred and fifty rooms, built as a fashionable adaptation of a traditional regional style. The architect, Roger Seassal, was a previous winner of the Grand Prix de Rome. As Juan-les-Pins was a stone's throw from Cap d'Antibes, Frank Jay Gould was certain that he could entice the illustrious guests down the road to the town he would create out of nothing. Taking inspiration from similar schemes in Florida and the west coast of America, he laid plans for several building plots on a grid system, separated by straight avenues, and also incorporating some parkland and plots of the pine trees that gave the town its name. The success was immediate—Frank Jay Gould himself was surprised at the speed with which his resort took off. Such famous names as Picasso, Marie Laurencin, Rebecca West, and Jean Cocteau came to see the new town for themselves. Scott Fitzgerald also succumbed to the temptation, often making the short journey down the road to look in at the Hotel Provençal, until the famous night when he forced the hotel orchestra to play to him all night in his Villa Saint Louis. He locked them into his bedroom and threw the key out of the window!

the gods arrive **85**

The Promenade des Anglais in Nice, circa 1929. On the right is the Palais de la Méditerranée, converted into a casino by the architects Charles and Dalmas.

The entrance lobby to the Palais de la Méditerranée. The grandiose staircase gives an indication of the sumptuous decor to be found inside.

The creation of Juan-les-Pins as a holiday resort marked the absolute conquest of the Riviera by the Americans. They brought their own lifestyle and unique architecture, which gradually came to dominate the entire coast, giving rise to innumerable buildings in a style which can only be described as "American beach resort Art Deco." Whole towns like Ste. Maxime, Toulon, and Hyères still bear the imprint of this rather elegant style. To this day, anyone walking along the sea front in one of these towns can admire the vestiges of these buildings, which so often look as if they really belong in other climes.

To give an example of the craze for all things American, the great couturier Paul Poiret, a star in the roaring twenties, the man who rid women of corsets forever, wanted to pay homage to the new trend. He chose to present his new summer collection in a set inspired by New York, against a backdrop of silhouettes of skyscrapers and accompanied by wailing police sirens.

Larger than Life

Although the Fitzgeralds, the Murphys, and the rest of the first wave of trend-setting visitors who discovered the Riviera after the First World War were soon to abandon their villas, never to return, the Côte d'Azur was about to welcome a new and equally artistic set, lured by the promise of sunshine. They were actors and film directors, members of the "café society," the original and much more entertaining version of today's jet set.

As early as 1924, the film director Rex Ingram persuaded Metro Goldwyn Mayer to consider using the Victorine studios, which were soon seen as a kind of miniature Hollywood. It was hoped that the climatic conditions would prove similar enough to those on America's west coast to give the same results. With little or no rain for ten months out of twelve, it was possible to film nearly all year round. Rex Ingram, part of the Murphy-Fitzgerald set, first came to the south of France to film *The Four Horsemen of the Apocalypse*, starring Rudolph Valentino. He entirely revitalized the Victorine studios, where business had been fairly slow since they were founded in 1918. He was only the first of many film directors to come to the Riviera: he was followed by Marcel L'Herbier for the first version of his *Diable au Corps* in 1926, Maurice Gleize for *The Madonna of the Sleeping Cars*, and Jean Renoir with *Marquitta*—all classics of the silent era. The most famous production to come out of the Victorine studios was without a doubt Marcel Carné's *Les Enfants du Paradis*, filmed during the Second World War. Many of the film crew were Jewish refugees working under false names. The Victorine went into a terminal decline in the 1950s and 1960s. In 1972 François Truffaut made one last attempt to save it by filming *La Nuit Américaine* there, but in vain.

The Villa Fiesole, Cannes
and a view of the Faun Staircase.

Isadora Duncan is still a
legend on the Côte d'Azur. She
died tragically, in front of
the Negresco, strangled
by her own scarf.

Josephine Baker
in Antibes in 1925.

Meanwhile, other luminaries from the world of film were arriving on the coast. Charlie Chaplin, Norma Shearer, and Erich von Stroheim were among the first, provoking hysteria among their fans. There is a charming anecdote about Charlie Chaplin's time on the Riviera. He was a great admirer of Maurice Maeterlinck, author of *The Bluebird*, and was thrilled to dine with him at his villa one day. Maeterlinck had purchased a magnificent villa at the foot of Mont Boron in Nice, which was originally designed as a casino. (Today, the Palais Maeterlinck is a luxury hotel, where the salons are said to be as large as the church La Madeleine in Paris.) On leaving the villa, Charlie Chaplin decided to go for a stroll. A young lady recognized him and rushed to request an autograph. He willingly signed his name for her, with a large smile — but when the young lady took the paper back, she exclaimed, "Oh no, please sign it 'Charlot'!" Charlie Chaplin was taken aback, and replied, "Charlot? Who is Charlot?" And so, quite by chance, he discovered the name by which he was known to millions of French admirers.

The Riviera also attracted other artists. Henri Matisse was one of them. He arrived at the end of the First World War, and often used young and pretty aspiring actresses as models for his paintings. Here, in Nice, he found the sort of light and dramatic scenery he had been looking for all his life, which corresponded to the shape of his dreams.

Apart from a brief stay in the Villa des Alliés in 1918, he deliberately refused to put down roots, preferring to move from one hotel to another, setting up astonishing workshops in each. He led a nomad lifestyle, moving from the Hotel Beaurivage, to the Hotel de la Méditerranée, where he stayed from 1918 to 1921, to a superb apartment opposite the flower market in Nice. He finally decided to settle down at the Regina, the former residence of Queen Victoria, on the Cimiez hills overlooking the town, on the advice of his doctor, who said he should avoid the sea air. Henri Matisse was especially fond of the Hotel de la Méditerranée. His friend Francis Carco later wrote a book in which he recorded Matisse's impressions of the hotel:

> An old and decent hotel, of course! And such pretty
> Italian-style ceilings! What tiles! They shouldn't have
> demolished the building. I stayed there for four years
> for the pleasure of painting. Do you remember the
> light that shone through the shutters? Everything was
> fake, absurd, amazing, delicious..."

He painted some true masterpieces during these years: *The Draughts Game, The Music Lesson,* and *The Dance,* a homage to his friendship with Diaghilev. In the early 1920s, he collaborated with the great choreographer on the set design for the ballet *The Song of the Nightingale*.

Another wonderful artist who was a leading member of the artistic scene on the Riviera in the roaring twenties was Jean-Gabriel Domergue. In

Menton.
The seafront promenade.

The Serres de la Madone estate in Menton.
Lawrence Johnston, a British army major gassed
during the First World War, created this famous
garden.

1926, he built a magnificent residence, the Villa
Fiesole, in Cannes. (He left it to the city after his
death, when it was renamed the Villa Domergue in
his honor.) It was based on the great Florentine
palaces of the Renaissance that he admired so much.
He was brilliant and urbane, and delighted in
organizing splendid parties, some of which have
gone down in history, like the party he threw in 1929
for the French singer Maurice Chevalier, then living
in the Villa La Louque, near Cannes. Jean-Gabriel
Domergue was much in demand as a portrait painter,
and many 1920s legends sat for him: Josephine
Baker, Mrs. Frank Jay Gould, Lady Owen, and the
Dolly Sisters, a pair of Hungarian-American twins
who were, for a while, the lovers of Gordon
Selfridge, the department store magnate. Domergue's
work is a fascinating depiction, not just of individual
beauties, but of the spirit of a whole era.

Two other flamboyant characters must be
mentioned in the history of artistic life on the Riviera
in the 1920s. Francis Picabia was already well-known
in artistic circles in America for driving the early Dada
movement, in collaboration with Man Ray, and he was
to remain faithful to his iconoclastic, nonconformist
image back in France as well. He had a passion for
two things—coupé sports cars and women, collecting
both indifferently. Once, he purchased a plot of land
near Cannes and installed a fake cemetery so that he
could snap up the neighboring plots cheaply when
the owners sold up in a hurry.

The other star who made her mark on the Côte
d'Azur was the Irish-American dancer, Isadora
Duncan. She came back to the coast around 1920
after her separation from Paris Singer, now married
to the great poet of the Russian revolution, Sergei
Essenin, who tragically committed suicide in 1925.
Isadora, preferring Rolls Royces to trams, had soon
tired of Moscow society, and returned to the south
of France. Her experience in post-revolution Russia
had inspired her briefly to proclaim the wonders of
Communism, and she insisted to the porter of the
Grand Hotel in St.-Jean-Cap-Ferrat, where she was
staying, that she was indeed a Bolshevik. Eventually,
she opened a dance school in Nice. Because she only
taught children, she now announced to anyone who
would listen that she was no longer a Communist,
but a pederast... respecting the true etymological
sense of both words, of course. She bore deep
psychological scars as a result of the death of her
children, and one evening when she had drunk
rather too much champagne, she tried to drown
herself in the Mediterranean. She was saved in the
nick of time by a retired British army officer, and
suffered nothing worse than a case of pneumonia. To
celebrate the end of her convalescence, one of her
friends offered to take her for a drive. Isadora liked
to dress lightly, in costumes inspired by ancient
Greek dancers, and her gentleman friend suggested
she put on something warmer to protect her from
the chilly night air. She refused a coat, which would

The Villa Mauresque, in St.-Jean-Cap-Ferrat, belonged to Somerset Maugham. It was a real refuge for the author, who spent many years of his long life here.

William Somerset Maugham. The celebrated author settled in St.-Jean-Cap-Ferrat in 1926.

have spoiled her outfit, but accepted a long silk scarf instead. A few minutes later, she waved merrily to her friends from the front seat of the Bugatti parked in front of the Negresco, crying "Farewell! I go to glory!" Then, as the car started, her scarf became entangled in the wheels, instantly breaking her neck.

Tea Beneath the Palm Trees

Meanwhile, the British had not abandoned the Riviera completely. Their presence was perhaps more discreet than in the glory days of the *belle époque*, and they now formed a small, select world of their own alongside the brasher, more glitzy Americans. They could be divided into three main groups, exactly as in the nineteenth century: those who came to the Riviera for their health; the flamboyant aristocrats who flitted from one holiday spot to another; and those who were just passing through. The first group consisted of large numbers of people afflicted with tuberculosis, for whom the Riviera represented the last chance to regain their health. Thanks to its exceptional climate—frost is unknown there—the town of Menton was practically transformed into a giant open-air sanatorium. Two visitors, very different in character, left their mark on the town.

First was Katherine Mansfield, who rented the Villa Isola Bella in 1920. The young New Zealand author had first come to the south of France a few

years earlier, just after her beloved brother was killed in service in 1915. The southern sun had proved a balm to her broken heart, allowing her to rise from the ashes of despair. During that first stay she wrote *Prelude*, in which she developed a favorite theme of constant renewal. When she returned to Menton, it was in the hope that the miracle would repeat itself, and that the sun would once again heal her. Her journal on September 1920 gives a taste of the pleasure she felt at being in the sun again:

> *Breakfast time. It grew hot. Everywhere the light quivered green-gold. The white soft road unrolled, with plane-trees casting a trembling shade. There were piles of pumpkins and gourds: outside the house the tomatoes were spread in the sun. Blue flowers and red flowers and tufts of deep purple flared in the road-side hedges... We bought figs for breakfast, immense thin-skinned ones. They broke in one's fingers and tasted of wine and honey.*

But this time, her sickness was physical, not spiritual. She wrote and wrote to exorcise the specter of the consumption that was to kill her. During her time in Menton she produced some of her finest stories, and seems to have found a kind of inner peace and tranquility. Like Edith Wharton in her convent, Katherine Mansfield felt that the Villa Isola Bella was the only place in the world for her, and it was here that she spent the happiest hours of her short life. She felt that if she could not conquer her illness here, she would not manage to do so

An aviation meeting in Monaco.
Photograph by J.-H. Lartigue, 1922.

Juan-les-Pins in 1928,
and the seaplane that linked Nice to the
other resorts on the Côte d'Azur.

Coco Chanel with the interior designer
Christian Bérard and the artist Boris Kochno in
Monte Carlo in 1932.

Coco Chanel.

Fashion on the Côte d'Azur.
A contemporary fashion magazine.

Coco Chanel
with Marcelle Meyer on
board a yacht belonging to
the Duke of Westminster.

anywhere. Yet the sickness was too strong, and she passed away less than two years later. She often used to say that, when she died, Isola Bella would be engraved on her heart. Her beloved villa is now a museum, and the New Zealand government has installed a plaque in her memory on the wall. Katherine Mansfield was not the only great writer to die of tuberculosis in the region. D.H. Lawrence, author of *Lady Chatterley's Lover*, died of the disease in Vence, in 1930.

A certain Major Lawrence Johnston also came to settle in the town at exactly this time. He was the new owner of the Serres de la Madone, a large estate in the Italian style, with a terraced park. Major Johnston was the designer of the famous gardens at Hidcote Manor in Gloucestershire. Like Katherine Mansfield, he moved to the south of France for the sake of his health; his lungs had been damaged in a gas attack during the war. At once he saw that the wonderful climate would finally allow him to create the garden of his dreams. Following the example of Thomas Hanbury at La Mortola, the major adapted a large number of subtropical plants to the Mediterranean climate to create one of the loveliest gardens on the coast, designed to be in flower all year round. Major Johnston was so dedicated to his garden that he would think nothing of going halfway round the world, as far as China, to bring back varieties of rare plants which could never have survived in his Cotswolds garden. He was a witty, urbane, slightly

eccentric gentleman, who delighted in showing important visitors round the different levels of his garden, his many dachshunds at their heels.

William Somerset Maugham also deserves a mention in this section, although by the time he came to live in St.-Jean-Cap-Ferrat in 1926 he was totally cured of the tuberculosis that had nearly cost him his life. He had won worldwide fame with the publication of his *Of Human Bondage* in 1915—one of the great twentieth-century novels. Somerset Maugham was in fact born in France, as his father was employed at the British Embassy in Paris at the time of his son's birth in 1874. The renowned author and former secret agent was irresistibly drawn to the colorful world of the Riviera, so different from the stilted, repressed atmosphere of upper-class drawing rooms back in Britain. On the Riviera he was beyond the reach of British laws, and could live with his lover Gerald Paxton—declared *persona non grata* in London—in all liberty. It was because of his declared homosexuality that Somerset Maugham was never knighted for his services to the crown, even though he was the biggest-selling author of his generation, along with Dame Agatha Christie. One day, Somerset Maugham discovered a neglected old villa which he was able to purchase for a song. The Villa Mauresque was a folly from the early years of the century, whose design he gradually transformed to a neo-classical one. From then on, although Somerset Maugham still traveled widely in Asia, his

Designs for evening gowns, by Coco Chanel.

Designs for evening gowns, by Coco Chanel.

Virginia Woolf was one of the few who disliked the Côte d'Azur.

Rudyard Kipling.

The Villa Les Bruyères, in St.-Jean-Cap-Ferrat, belonged to the Duke of Connaught, another of Queen Victoria's sons.

home was the villa, and St.-Jean-Cap-Ferrat. He did think for a while that he was not going to be able to stay, however, because after years of words just flowing from his pen, he was struck with writer's block. At first he was worried by this unusual lack of concentration, until he realized that he was simply distracted by the magnificent view from his desk, which stood right in front of a window overlooking the bay of Villefranche. His muse returned only once he covered the window. Some of Somerset Maugham's best and most famous works are set on the Côte d'Azur, such as the short story with the telling title, *The Three Fat Women of Antibes*, and the novel *The Razor's Edge*, in which the characters play out their destiny along this stretch of coast.

Although the Riviera was not as elegant now as it once had been, there were still crowds of British aristocrats who were not too proud to taste its pleasures, following the examples of their parents and grandparents. Eugène Cornuché's associate François André was particularly keen to entice them—and their lavish spending habits—to the coast. While the brilliant Eugène Cornuché was luring guests to the casino in Cannes with free holidays, François thought of another, equally brilliant, stratagem to draw the attention of the Chelsea and Mayfair set. His idea was to inaugurate the first direct air link from England to the coast, starting in 1927. A plane left Croydon at dawn with two hundred copies each of *The Times* and the *Daily*

Telegraph on board, to be sold that evening on the Croisette in Cannes. Since there was no airport in Nice at the time, the plane landed in Marignane, further down the coast, and the papers were brought in to town by seaplane. For the newspapers to be in Cannes before nightfall, the first plane had to land at Marignane by half-past three in the afternoon. In the early days of aviation, this was asking the impossible; the primitive motors of the period were hardly guaranteed to beat fog and frost. The pilots managed to arrive on time only twice in one month. It was calculated that the four hundred newspapers cost François André one hundred thousand francs, but the free publicity generated by the scheme was worth much more.

The bay at Cannes was a popular mooring spot for yachts. Two of the biggest belonged to friendly rivals, the immensely wealthy Lady Furness and the Duke and Duchess of Westminster, who always moored alongside one another in an attempt to show each other up. The family of the Duke of Westminster owned half of London—as it still does today. The duke and duchess had a son who fell madly in love with Coco Chanel. Hoping to win her heart, he bought her a huge mansion, La Pausa, in Cap Martin, and asked for her hand in marriage. But Coco was not to be swayed. Fiercely independent, she refused his proposal, saying "There have been many Duchesses of Westminster, but only one Coco Chanel!"

The Cubist garden designed by Guévrekian
for the Villa Noailles, Hyères.

The lounge room of the Villa Noailles, owned by
Charles and Marie-Laure de Noailles. They entertained
the most important avant-garde artists of the day.

It was not only idle aristocrats who enjoyed life in
the sun. The Riviera was also a favorite destination
for many eminent politicians and their families.
Lloyd George came for the founding conference of
the League of Nations, and the Balfours and Curzons
also came. Even a few Indian maharajahs made the
trip. Lady Asquith, wife of the former prime minister
Herbert Asquith, was one woman who really stood
out from the crowd as a figure of utter elegance. She
loved haute couture, and in the early years of the
century had won over French hearts, while causing a
minor diplomatic incident, by helping the couturier
Paul Poiret open a boutique in the center of London,
before the signature of the Entente Cordiale.

Another typically British eccentric to be seen on
the coast at this time was one of Queen Victoria's
many children, the Duke of Connaught. He
purchased the Villa Les Bruyères in St.-Jean-Cap-
Ferrat in 1921. There he led the old-fashioned life of
a country gentleman, taking a stroll at the same time
every day and ordering his gardeners to remove all
exotic plants from his flowerbeds.

Some visitors to the Riviera came through
curiosity, to see why the place was so fashionable.
Rudyard Kipling came to Hyères for a few weeks in
1921 and 1923. Virginia Woolf, suffering from
depression, spent some time in Cassis with her
sister, who had come to paint. Virginia was at first
charmed by the landscape, the narrow creeks along
the coast and the blinding white rocks plunging
straight into the sapphire sea, but she rapidly tired
of the incredible monotony of the social life—the
same faces, the same Rolls Royces, the same caviar,
and always the unvarying pulse of the waves... Her
stay made one lasting impression on her, however,
when a moth flew into an oil lamp and was
consumed, inspiring her to write one of her most
important novels, *The Waves.* The Riviera had shown
Virginia Woolf the absolute futility of individual
lives and the vital, cosmic force that rules us all, as it
had done for Katherine Mansfield—whom Virginia
considered her only rival—a few years before.

Old and New

How did Edith Wharton feel about this invasion of
the coast, which had been such a tranquil refuge for
her only a few years before? The people now arriving
on the Riviera were an unfamiliar breed to her, and
she found them of little interest. She was only mildly
entertained by the ready-made art of Marcel
Duchamp—for example, a white porcelain urinal
exhibited unaltered except for the addition of a
signature and the title *Fountain*. Edith Wharton, an
expert in implicit, unspoken sentiments, felt that this
new generation was too open and quick to reveal all

A still from the *Mystery of the Château of Dice*, directed by
Man Ray at the Villa Noailles.
The title was inspired by the
villa's geometrical forms.

Marie-Laure and Charles de Noailles
in evening dress.

A still from Man Ray's film,
The Mystery of the Château of Dice.

Man Ray during the filming of *The Mystery of the Château of Dice.*

The terrace of the Villa Noailles. Among the guests are Boris Kochno, Pierre Colle, Igor Markevitch, Francis Poulenc, Luis Buñuel, Christian Bérard, Alberto Giacometti—all friends of Marie-Laure and Charles de Noailles.

The Villa Noailles, Hyères,
designed by Robert Mallet-Stevens for
Charles de Noailles. In the background the
ruins of the old convent can be seen.

its feelings. After a lifetime studying the ways of a
stable, unchanging, seemingly eternal elite, she was
now confronted with a younger generation who was
only too aware of the terrible brevity of human
existence. Edith had lost her beloved father at a
young age, but she had accepted this as a personal
blow of fate, feeding the slightly masochistic
emotional attitude that was the key to her inner
world. She built her world on memories. The
Fitzgeralds and the other stars that shone too
brightly wished only to forget and enjoy the moment.

It is characteristic of Edith that, like the first
generation of visitors, she in fact preferred the

Riviera in the winter. She always found the fashion
for spending the summer on the coast a little vulgar,
and continued to spend the hottest months of the
year in her home near Paris.

Edith's neighbors in Hyères were a wealthy and
aristocratic couple, famed as major patrons of the
arts, Charles and Marie-Laure de Noailles. They had
moved in to a nearby villa, which was to become the
Villa Noailles, in 1923, and had much in common
with their celebrated neighbor—a distinguished
family background, a sure eye for the arts, and a great
love of gardens. The de Noailles were at the forefront
of the avant-garde, and had their new home entirely

The Villa Noailles was a famous
centre for avant-garde art in the 1930s.

redesigned by Mallet-Stevens, who gave the building a resolutely modernist look. Their home was open to all the young stars of the avant-garde who were having such a profound effect on the art world: André Breton, Salvador Dali, Man Ray (who made the first Surrealist film, *The Mystery of the Château of Dice* here, in 1929), Luis Buñuel (author of the *Golden Age*) and, above all, Jean Cocteau. The de Noailles provided financial backing for Cocteau's first film, *The Blood of a Poet*. At the time, Cocteau was staying at the Hotel Welcome in nearby Villefranche, and left much evidence of his creative genius in the region, which was a well of inspiration to him. Examples are the

frescoes in the Chapelle Saint Pierre in Villefranche and the decoration of the Villa Santo Sospir in St.-Jean-Cap-Ferrat, belonging to Francine Weisweiller—he liked to say he had "tattooed the walls" there.

What did Edith Wharton think of this hard-nosed modernist movement, with its new artistic notions? She had very little in common with it, truth to tell, and she was never able to become very close to her bohemian neighbors—although she was very great friends with the poet Anna de Noailles, from the same family. She preferred another one of her neighbors, Lawrence Johnston, whose philosophy on life was much closer to hers. The pair spent many

The ballet *Blue Train* called on a number of talented
participants including Jean Cocteau, Coco Chanel,
Darius Milhaud, Pablo Picasso, and Sergei Diaghilev.

A scene from the ballet, *Blue Train.*

An advertising poster designed by Charles Hallo, specially created to appeal to the British holidaymaker.

A poster designed by Pierre Zenoble.
In 1928, the Blue Train introduced sleeper
cars for its British clients.

happy hours planning the gardens of Edith's two homes in France. Major Johnston came up with a design that allied the twin concepts of serenity and a pleasant sense of unfamiliarity. Such sensations had always been vital to preserve Edith's sense of wellbeing, even more so now that she was approaching old age. Many of her friends and acquaintances were no longer with her, in particular her beloved cousin, and some say lover, Walter Berry, who had recently suffered a fatal stroke. Edith's love of gardening was becoming a real passion, as if her stewardship of the landscape gave her some sort of fleeting control over the passage of time and the seasons. Otherwise, how to explain her bout of anguished depression when a terrible blizzard killed many of her trees and plants in 1929? She lamented the death of her garden, seeing in it a harbinger of her own passing.

Yet even at this difficult time, the Riviera worked its magic once more, soothing Edith's nerves and giving her the energy to maintain her mental equilibrium. And although she did not adopt the new tendencies that were sweeping the Riviera—everything from Surrealism and Dadaism to high-cut bathing costumes—she was certainly far from being cut off from her surroundings. Not without reason had her old friend and mentor Henry James compared her to a pendulum and to a firebird, a phoenix reborn from its own ashes. Though in her autobiography, *A Backward Glance*, she laments the passing of time, now she simply got on with life. Back in Hyères in 1926, she had the idea for a new literary prize. The first winner was a rising star, the novelist Anita Loos. Edith even went so far as to declare that Loos had written a novel that would go down in the annals of literary history, the best novel since the eighteenth-century classic *Manon Lescaut*. Its title— *Gentlemen Prefer Blondes*.

It was at this time that Edith Wharton, ever driven by the need to seduce, was to live two last great friendships, the special sort of semi-platonic, semi-romantic relationship with younger men she had enjoyed so often in her life. The two men were writers, they gave a new lease of life to her own flagging spirit. One was Bernard Berenson, the other was a close neighbor living in Sanary, the author of the classic *Brave New World*, Aldous Huxley, a man few would accuse of being backward-looking.

BATAILLES
DE FLEURS

Les Batailles de Fleurs de Cannes,
données dans un cadre unique, réu-
nissent pour ces charmants tournois
les personnalités les
plus connues parmi
nos hôtes assidus.

Au centre de cette page
les DOLLY SISTERS
sourient à travers les
roses.

Photos Feneyrol

the house of mirth
(1930...)

The Palm Beach Casino, Cannes,
was the place to be seen.

The Palm Beach Casino, Cannes,
as seen from the beach.

And suddenly, the world came tumbling down...

October 23, 1929: the Wall Street crash. Stock prices had been overheating for a while and now came crashing down. On Black Thursday, thousands of people lost entire fortunes in a matter of minutes. The whole world was soon rocked by the crisis. In New York, many people committed suicide rather than face ruin. The political situation in France was also perilous; there had recently been the Marthe Hanau scandal (the famous banker had a number of ministers and members of parliament in her pocket, but her bank collapsed nonetheless) and the Stavisky affair (a swindler with friends in high places) which undermined the credibility of the government. Mussolini had taken power in Italy and Hitler was about to do the same in Germany. The world was still recovering from the massacres of the First World War, and seemed to be afflicted by some terrible sickness blighting its chances of a prosperous and peaceful future.

The Riviera was, of course, a symbol of the *nouveaux riches*, of easy money, of a glamorous and cosmopolitan lifestyle. It should have been one of the first places to feel the shock-waves of the collapse of the American stock exchange. The investors who were still building magnificent luxury hotels and new casinos like the Palm Beach (named after the Florida resort) in towns like Cannes were indeed taking a great risk with their money.

And yet, nothing really changed. Some familiar faces disappeared from the scene to nurse their wounds in private, but in general, life was still the party it had always been for these fortunate few. Maybe the general air of insouciance on the Riviera was due to a desire to make the best of life while it was still possible, or to a feeling that those who had come out of the crisis unscathed were now beyond danger, that nothing could harm them. Despite the crisis of 1929—or maybe in part because of it—Juan-les-Pins, Antibes, and Cap d'Antibes became more popular than ever with Americans. They drew an eclectic crowd of jazz musicians and newly wealthy businessmen who had taken advantage of the crash to make their fortune. Famous faces were everywhere, on the Croisette, in Monte Carlo, or on the Promenade des Anglais. People were already making fun of a certain type of lady often seen in the vicinity, who refused to grow old gracefully, strutting along the beach in revealing outfits designed for someone thirty years younger. In the early 1930s, the Riviera was truly the only place to be.

Party Time

Despite the fact that Monte Carlo had become an emblematic town—in 1930 Paramount even produced a film, *Monte Carlo*, directed by Ernst Lubitsch—American visitors now congregated in Cannes, just down the road from Antibes. As a result, the private

Fun and games at the Palm Beach.

Ella Fitzgerald and Duke Ellington in
Juan-Les-Pins. One of the highlights of the season.

The European Jazz Festival
at Juan-Les-Pins.

Palm Beach Casino in Cannes became the place to be seen, superseding the municipal casino run by Eugène Cornuché and François André, which was originally a winter attraction. The Palm Beach became the first summer casino on the coast. After his triumph in Juan-les-Pins, the architect Roger Seassal was called upon to design the new casino. He was given carte blanche, and came up with a stupendous design to be built at the very end of the Croisette. The final result was astonishing: a mixture of Venetian palace and the Alhambra, resembling a fantastic set straight out of the Victorine studios.

The Palm Beach officially opened on April 5, 1929. Henri Rülh, the owner and manager, hired a jazz band for the festivities. This new style of music was an immediate hit, and before long Louis Armstrong and Sidney Bechet were invited to perform their magic on the Riviera. The day after the official opening, the American newspapers reported that the Palm Beach was the most splendid casino in the world. It hosted party after party, including the magnificent gala held to celebrate, for the first time on French soil, American Independence Day. It fulfilled every wish: an open-air salt-water swimming pool, where bathing beauties could be seen vaunting their charms, a stage, and of course the gaming tables. It was open night and day, and the jet set loved it. Charlie Chaplin, Maurice Chevalier, and the Rothschilds were just some of the famous faces to be spotted having a flutter at one of the tables.

The Palm Beach was such a smash hit that before long the town hall was obliged to take steps to regulate the traffic—mainly limousines—and to install electric lighting along the Croisette. Its success reached dizzying heights in 1936, when the newspaper *Le Jour* decided to transfer its famous annual charity ball in favor of children with tuberculosis from Paris to the new casino. In a strange twist of history, the town that had been launched by Lord Brougham, looking for a spot for his consumptive daughter to convalesce, was now to play a key part in the fight against the disease. Two thousand guests paid a thousand francs each to watch a show by such stars of the French stage and concert hall as Gaby Morlay, Jean Sablon, Serge Lifar, and the ever-popular Tino Rossi. Some of the best-known fashion designers of the day, including Jeanne Lanvin, Elsa Schiaparelli, Jacques Heim, Maguy Rouff, and Madeleine Vionnet, donated items for the grand tombola that was to be the highlight of the evening. The event was covered live by several radio stations, including an American one. The Palm Beach was now a legend on two continents.

The early years of the 1930s were also a golden age for the Monte Carlo casino, which now employed over five hundred croupiers. The American billionaire Vanderbilt once won over six million francs (over three million in today's euros) in one night. The lure of gold is hard to resist, even for a billionaire...

Bibi at the Palais de la Méditerranée,
Nice, 1929. Photograph by J.-H. Lartigue.

Opposite:
Dancing at the Hotel Ruhl in Nice.
Photograph by J.-H. Lartigue, 1929.

the house of mirth **115**

Josephine Baker and friends on the terrace
at the Palais de la Méditerranée, Nice, 1932.

Coco Chanel and Serge Lifar
on the Côte d'Azur.

Mr. and Mrs. Simpson

Just as Queen Victoria had been a frequent visitor to
the Côte d'Azur in the late nineteenth century, now
her great-grandson, Edward, Prince of Wales, came
to taste its delights. But times had changed, and
there was an aura of scandal around the prince's
visits that would have been unthinkable in his great-
grandmother's day. He did not trouble to hide his
infatuation with a twice-divorced American lady by
the name of Wallis Simpson. The story of the man
who gave up a kingdom for love is well known. The
couple chose to come to the Riviera to live one of
the century's great love affairs, which forced a king
into exile. In 1934, in the early days of their affair,
Edward and Wallis decided to go on a cruise on the
Mediterranean to escape unwanted press attention
and the frankly hostile court. They were charmed by
the atmosphere of the French resorts, and rented
the Villa le Roc in Golfe Juan to spend the following
summer together in private. Back in England, their
behavior was much frowned upon. It has to be said
that the photographs of the couple that reached
London were hardly of the sort to set people's
minds at rest. They showed the Prince of Wales, heir
to the throne, having fun in the sun in a most un-
Royal manner. Given that England was experiencing
a difficult social climate, Edward's behavior was
perhaps ill-judged. As for the haughty and highly
elegant Mrs. Simpson, politicians accused her of
seeing the crown already within her grasp. Sir Henry
Channon wrote in his diary that she already had the
air of someone who expected people to bow as she
entered the room, or at least would not have been
surprised had they done so. While the couple was
trying to escape the barrage of criticism in the south
of France, Edward was preparing his riposte. He
invited Lloyd George and Winston Churchill to visit
him to discuss the situation. They were unyielding,
and it became a battle of wills between the Prince of
Wales and the House of Commons.

When the story became public, and Edward, now
king, finally lost the battle, Wallis Simpson sought
refuge in Cannes. Here, on December 11th, 1936, she
listened to Edward's abdication speech on the radio.
He was abdicating because it was impossible for him
to reign "without the help and support of the
woman I love." Wallis was staying with some friends
of hers, the Rodgers, at the Villa Lou Viei. She had
to face the opprobrium of the old-fashioned winter
guests alone. Queen Maud of Norway summed up
the general feeling on the coast, saying, "I hear that
in Monte Carlo, all the English and French leave as
soon as she walks in... I wish something bad would
befall her!"

However, while Wallis was being given the cold
shoulder by all Europe's nobility, she was adulated
in her home country. Loathed in Britain, the woman
from Baltimore became the darling of America, the
living symbol of the nation's dream of success. One

The Château de la Croë,
between Juan-les-Pins and
Antibes, was built for a couple of
English aristocrats in 1930. In
Summer 1938, Wallis and Edward
moved in. They redecorated the
entire château, giving rise to what
is known as the Windsor style.

anecdote in particular shows just how popular the
couple was in the United States: not one single
telephone call was made in New York while Edward
VIII was announcing his abdication (the British
claimed he had acquired a dreadful American accent
since he had picked up with that Simpson woman).
It is hard to imagine an event that could bring such
an expectant hush to a city today!

This incredible wave of support brought the Duke
and Duchess of Windsor back to the Riviera, this
time for the summer season. Here, at least, they were
guaranteed a welcome befitting their station. They
spent summer 1938 at the Château de la Cröe, a
stone's throw from Juan-les-Pins and Cap d'Antibes.
The château was a superb, immense white house with
a circular peristyle, built by an English aristocrat and
his wife in 1930. With a huge swimming pool blasted
out of the bare rock and its four hectares of pine
forest running down to the sea, it was the perfect
refuge for the couple: isolated, yet elegant enough to
welcome a few select visitors. The Windsors began to
frequent the jet set, bathing, drinking champagne,
enjoying themselves so as to forget that elsewhere,
they were spurned. The duchess even tried her hand
at a new sport that was all the rage—water skiing
(invented on the bay at Juan-les-Pins)—as if to prove
that she wasn't afraid of anything.

As the Windsors had taken a lease until 1949,
they decided to redecorate the entire house. The

famous Windsor style was beginning to emerge, and
would reach its most perfect expression after the
Second World War in their magnificent home in
Bagatelle, near Paris. The duke brought over
furnishings from Fort Belvedere and from his
former homes in England. Gradually, they gathered
a close circle of friends—a new "court"—around
them, including Somerset Maugham, Churchill,
Barbara Hutton, the Cabrols, the Polignacs, and the
Duff Coopers. Somerset Maugham had been a
particular friend of the duchess ever since she had
spent some weekends at his villa during her earlier
"exile" in Cannes.

The man who had given up his throne for love
often used to walk about in his kilt, and enjoyed
improvising concerts on his bagpipes. He insisted
that his wife be addressed as "Your Royal Highness,"
a title to which she in fact had no claim. As for the
duchess, she was often seen in outfits of a rare
elegance, designed by Mainbocher, and vied to be on
the covers of magazines with the queen of
Hollywood, Marlene Dietrich, come from Beverly
Hills to try a new experience—sunbathing. Local
newspapers were delighted, and ran huge headlines
saying "The Blue Angel changes color!" A little later,
Hollywood was back again, this time in the persons
of Claudette Colbert and Gary Cooper, who had
come to the Riviera to star in Ernst Lubitsch's latest
comedy, *Bluebeard's Eighth Wife*.

A still from *Bluebeard's Eighth Wife*,
directed by Ernst Lubitsch.

MAC-MAHON DISTRIBUTION présente

LA HUITIEME FEMME DE BARBE BLEUE
une grande comédie américaine de ERNST LUBITSCH
avec Gary COOPER et Claudette COLBERT

A French film poster for *Bluebeard's Eighth Wife,*
directed by Ernst Lubitsch.

LA HUITIEME FEMME DE BARBE BLEUE

une grande comédie américaine de ERNST LUBITSCH
avec Gary COOPER et Claudette COLBERT

A French film poster for *Bluebeard's Eighth Wife*,
directed by Ernst Lubitsch.

Legendary French
singer Edith Piaf on
her way to the Riviera.

Between Dreams and Reality

This small stretch of coast quickly took on the
qualities of a dream world, where anything was
possible. As well as the Windsors, other emblematic
figures made the Riviera their home. Among them
was the legendary French singer, Edith Piaf. Her
story was truly incredible. Born in a gutter in a Paris
slum, she started out as leader of her own gang
before taking her first step up the ladder to success,
selling violets outside the extremely chic café
Fouquet's. Before long, her astonishing voice and
good looks got her noticed by the couturier Paul
Poiret and the director of the Olympia music hall.
These two patrons gave her the name by which she
is now known—Piaf being French slang for sparrow,
in reference to her diminutive size. They also gave
her her first big break. However, at her first
appearance at the Olympia, the most celebrated
music hall in Paris, she was roundly booed. She was
not one to give up easily, though, and, frank and
outspoken as ever, shouted at the audience, "Well, if
you don't like my voice, have a look at my arse!" as
she bared her buttocks to them. There was an
immediate outcry, the show was a triumph from
then on, and Edith Piaf was hired to sing on
Broadway. There she married a South American
billionaire, Felicio Bénitez.

By the time she arrived on the Riviera, Edith Piaf
was a legend, rolling in wealth, and in particular the
owner of a fabulous collection of jewelry worth
several billion francs. She lived in a palatial
residence, the Villa Bagatelle, and had purchased
herself a British-sounding title, Countess Talbot. She
was not shy about displaying her riches—on the
contrary, she was inordinately proud of her success,
as well she might be—and often stayed on board her
yacht, the *Moineau IV*, which had more than thirty
guest rooms. As the name indicates, this was her
fourth yacht; Edith Piaf could never resist the
temptation to buy the latest model on the market.
She was given a post as cultural attaché to Santo
Domingo, which meant that she enjoyed the
advantages of diplomatic status and paid no tax. She
was a familiar figure in the casinos, such as that of
Monte Carlo, her favorite. She would often spend
entire nights there, playing with a huge pile of chips,
knowing that she could lose every night and still have
billions left. She lost none of her wicked sense of
humor, despite attaining fame and fortune. One day, a
tramp abused her in the street, threatening her with
some forthcoming revolution, to which she retorted,
"Yes, things are going to change. But I will be the
People's Commissioner, and you will still be a fool."

More poetic and certainly more romantic were
the visitors whose wealth was only matched by their
whimsy, who recreated private utopias worthy of a
Cecil B. DeMille film. For example, there was an
American couple, Henry and Mary Clews, who
acquired the Château de la Napoule, right by the

The Château de la Napoule.
This medieval folly was bought
by an American couple,
Henry and Mary Clews, who
recreated their own vision of a
medieval lifestyle there.

The garden at the Château de la Napoule,
a haven for millionaires and artists.

The Château de la Napoule and its
breathtaking view over the Mediterranean.

Mary and Henry Clews, in
the Château de la Napoule, where
guests were obliged to dress as if
at the Court of King Arthur.

French playwright, Sacha Guitry, at the train station in Cap d'Ail, 1929.

Sacha Guitry at the Grand Hotel, Cap d'Ail, Winter 1929.

sea, and rebuilt it entirely as a mock castle from an idealized medieval golden age, but with all the mod cons. The couple put their artistic and sculpting skills to good use to create a timeless, soothing atmosphere, and they often invited the *crème de la crème* of the art world to visit them in these surreal surroundings. Their guests were obliged to dress as if they were at the court of King Arthur, and many romantic moments were whiled away in the moonlight that flooded the garden, where Roman and Gothic windows in the wall gave magnificent views over the Mediterranean. The château has today been turned into a foundation for young artists from all over the world, and is open to visitors.

This world of extremes, of great beauty, great wit, and great wealth, where life was at once at its most modern and most fragile, seems so hermetic to us today that it can be a shock to remember that in fact it was open to influence from events in the world outside. One English countess in particular was deeply concerned about the introduction of the first paid holidays in 1936, for which the workers had fought long and hard. One day, she thought she spotted some workers on holiday—though they still were a rare breed—bathing in "her" spot. She called her butler in horror, and demanded that he install a bathtub on the beach, so she would not have to share the same water as the hoi polloi. However, the introduction of paid holidays on its own did not have very much impact on the tourist trade on the

coast. The real turning point came after the Second World War, when ever larger numbers of families acquired their first car.

After the crisis of 1929, the aftershocks of which lasted until the Second World War, fortunes continued to be made and lost. François Coty, the perfumer and newspaper magnate, lost his fortune in part due to his passion for gambling. Once, after a particularly hard night's gambling at the Monto Carlo casino, he quipped, "They say money has no smell. This time it's the smell that has no money." One of the clubs along the coast, the Paradise, made its name, if not its fortune, by organizing a high-kicking contest. The young American lady who won set a record by managing more than five thousand in a row. And yet, despite all of this frivolity, there was serious business going on behind the scenes. Several of the grand hotels hosted major international conferences at which the future of the world was discussed. It is not generally known that the political turmoil of the period was directly behind the idea, dreamed up in 1938, for a new annual film festival to be held in Cannes. It was deliberately created as a direct challenge to the success of the Venice Film Festival—known as Mostra—which enjoyed a rather too cozy relationship with the Italian and German fascist governments. The first edition of the Cannes Film Festival was planned for September 1939, and Philippe Erlanger was its first representative.

A storm on the seafront in Nice.
Photograph by J.-H. Lartigue.

The Battle of Flowers, Cannes, February 1933.
Photograph by J.-H. Lartigue.

Beaulieu. Women posing on the side of the road,
by the sea. Photograph by J.-H. Lartigue, 1921.

Vera at l'île de Saint-Honorat.
Photograph by J.-H. Lartigue, 1927.

The Second World War meant that the plans had to
be shelved until 1946, when the long-awaited festival
finally took place.

In 1938, Joseph Kennedy, American ambassador
in London, came to stay at the Château de
Beaumont with eight of his nine children, among
them a young John Fitzgerald. Officially, the family
was there on holiday. In fact, the real reason for
their presence was a secret meeting with Sir Walter
Elliot, the British Minister for the Colonies, and Mr.
Morgenthau, the American treasury secretary.
Joseph Kennedy was something of a dark horse, a
former film producer, lover of the Hollywood actress
Gloria Swanson, and the money behind Franklin D.
Roosevelt's presidential campaign. Now he was
trying to convince Washington of his fitness to serve
in a top government position. His deeply held
pacifist beliefs eventually cost him his career, when
he wanted to maintain America's neutral status
toward the end of the war. We now know that the
talk over the martinis on the beach was not just idle
gossip, but that the representative of the British
government was desperately trying to convince his
American counterparts of the imminence of the
danger, just before the Munich agreement was torn
up, heralding the outbreak of war.

But as the world slid inexorably towards war,
there was at least one cheerful event on the
horizon—the fairytale marriage of the Aga Khan to a
young French woman from the small fishing port of

Sète, farther along the coast towards Spain. Yvette
Labrousse was a famous beauty, elected Miss France
in 1930. The groom, His Highness Mohamed Aga
Khan III, a living god to over five hundred million
Ismailians, was a familiar figure on the Riviera. He
was a witty, urbane, and very refined gentleman,
who, since the late 1920s, divided most of his time
between Cannes and Deauville. A widower, his late
wife, a dancer at the theater in Monte Carlo, had left
him a son, Ali Khan. When he met Yvette, the
former beauty queen, she was running a small
couture house. They fell head over heels in love the
moment their eyes met. Yvette became the new
Begum, and the couple moved to the superb Villa
Yakimour (the name is a combination of the words
Yvette and *amour*) in Le Cannet.

Brave New World

As the Riviera became a playground for playboys
and princes, Edith Wharton withdrew into her
imagination. One of her favorite pastimes was
searching for beautiful out-of-the-way spots where
she could hold one of her splendid picnics. As the
years passed, she felt the need to organize such
excursions more and more often. She loved the
immensity of the blue sea, untouched by civilization:
here she felt she could somehow go back in time to
meet all her loved ones once more. Not by chance
did she write around this time an essay on Marcel

Edith Wharton. Rather shy, she lived a moderate life, drawing inspiration from the sensational lives of the people around her on the Côte d'Azur.

Proust, author of *In Remembrance of Things Past*, and one of her finest short stories, *After Holbein*, which is a magnificent portrait of a man staggering under the burden of time. Edith, filled with nostalgia for a dead past and fearful for a future which she felt held no place for her, found in nature the serenity she had longed for all her life. Still alone years after the end of her affair with Fullerton, she regretted her solitude, but knew in her heart that she had never truly desired to fall in love again—the first step to acceptance. Every man she had ever allowed to get close to her had been uncertain in his sexual identity. Edith dreamed of a flaming passion that would sweep her off her feet, but deep down she knew that she could not have borne such an experience—it would have cost her her muse. Her novel *The Age of Innocence*, which won the Pulitzer Prize in 1920, gives the exact measure of her frustration, which over the years proved such a rich well of inspiration. At the end of the novel, the heroine is offered the chance to experience such ardor, but decides instead to refuse and live her life without passion. Wisdom or folly? Edith preferred to enjoy the Mediterranean sun and forget.

And yet, the world she had found on her arrival on the Riviera was gone forever. Nothing in the brash, money-driven resorts spoke to her any more. The sort of soul-wrenching torments suffered by Henry James, or the silent, unquestioning subjection to duty that Edith had grown up with, seemed entirely alien in this society that delighted in rejecting the old rules and breaking taboos—the very rules which had governed and informed Edith's whole œuvre. Just in time, as all seemed lost for her, she was fortunate enough to become close with the two men already mentioned, the only people who from now on were to count in her eyes: Bernard Berenson and Aldous Huxley.

Aldous Huxley arrived in Sanary with his wife, Marie, in 1930, where the couple lived a rather private life, socializing only rarely. Aldous was a highly elegant man, and a close friend of D.H. Lawrence. He spent all his time working on his book, *Brave New World*, an apocalyptic vision of the future of humanity. He and Edith immediately became good friends, both sharing a taste for understatement and disillusioned pessimism, tempered with a good touch of humor. To begin with, Huxley found his august neighbor's "very New England" ways most amusing, and he treated her with a good-natured disrespect that no one had ever dared to display before. One day, he made her walk across her entrance hall while he pinched her buttocks all the way. Many of Edith's acquaintances were astonished at this familiar treatment, and even more so at the way Edith lapped it up—proof that they did not know her very well. It is true that she was ill-at-ease and stiff with people she did not know, but as soon as she felt at home, she was completely transformed. In her heart of hearts she

was still the strange, timid little girl, trembling as she waited in the vestibule of a grand New York mansion. Aldous Huxley filled Edith with nostalgia for her happiest childhood hours, spent in the nursery, not the drawing room. With him, she could allow herself to descend from her pedestal.

Bernard Berenson was a friend of long date, but they had grown particularly close since the death of Edith's beloved cousin, Walter Berry. Bernard did not live on the Riviera, preferring to spend his time in Italy, in his villa near Florence. Where Aldous was the lighthearted, jovial friend, Bernard's relationship with Edith was closer to that of a mentor and literary advisor. In fact, the friendship seems to have been all the stronger for having been mainly conducted by letter: they got on better when they did not spend too much time together. When Berenson came to visit, points of tension would suddenly arise from nowhere to crackle in the air. Edith's private secretary Nicky Mariano witnessed such scenes on several occasions. "Her relationship with B.B. was like that of a brother and a somewhat older sister... For the whole length of his visit, she would reproach him for taking such long siestas, which stole the best and sunniest hours." Once or twice, Nicky thought Edith was going too far in insisting on organizing one of her famous picnics, when her guest would much rather have stayed at home on the terrace. Bernard was not very keen on wandering the hillsides, off the beaten track. Surely Edith could have given up this

favorite hobby of hers for the two weeks or so of Bernard's visit? There are many points in common between Edith's relationships with these two men, Aldous and Bernard. What was the attraction? Boisterous comradeship, or a sense of what might have been, if only... Both men were a good deal younger than Edith, and they were both madly in love with their wives.

The tragedy of Edith Wharton's life was that her dual search for an impossible, perfect love and for her own roots made her modern before her time, and yet too old-fashioned to accept the form of modernity the world chose. This contradiction is at the heart of her work, and explains why she hoped to find a haven of peace on the Riviera, a region driven by its own paradoxes. Edith died just as the liberal, open society she had always struggled for was finally emerging—just a few years too late for her to adapt to the new ways.

And yet, shortly before her death in 1937, the Riviera witnessed the advent of something Edith Wharton had always dreamed of, a British civilization on the Mediterranean. The arrival en masse of the Americans during these years had put the British presence on the Riviera rather in the shade. Although His Majesty's subjects were perhaps not in the limelight, they were still quietly contributing to the unique lifestyle of this corner of France. Winston Churchill himself came to indulge in his passion for painting, producing many

Seaside fashion on the Côte d'Azur.

Seaside fashion on the Côte d'Azur.

The Villa Cypris in Cap Martin. The Moorish
pergola gives a fabulous view over the Mediterranean.

The famous pergola at the Villa Cypris in Cap Martin.

Somerset Maugham in his garden at the Villa
Mauresque in St.-Jean-Cap-Ferrat.

The wedding of Rita Hayworth and Ali Kahn, Vallauris, where the couple was given a warm welcome by the crowd. The reception was held at the Château Horizon, in Cap d'Antibes, with hundreds of guests in attendance.

watercolors of the view at Estérel. He had always been happiest when on the go, and even now moved constantly from hotel to hotel, from the Hotel de Paris in Monte Carlo to the Montfleury in Cannes. Wherever he stayed, he would leave large numbers of easels lying around the hotel, which must have been a trying experience for the hotel managers — but they put up with this whim admirably. Churchill had an artistic neighbor for a while in Pablo Picasso, who sincerely admired his work, advising him to give up politics and live by his brush! Picasso had first discovered the Riviera in 1919, and purchased the Villa Notre Dame de Vie near Mougins from the Guinness family.

Other creative souls from Great Britain and the recently independent Republic of Ireland also formed part of the Riviera community. There were William Butler Yeats, the great Irish poet, who lived a secluded life in Cap Martin; H. G. Wells, living a passionate and tumultuous love affair in Magnagocs; and Evelyn Waugh, the darling of society and biggest gossip of them all, in Villefranche.

Beyond their differences of geography and history, the British, Irish, and American communities lived side by side in groups that met and mingled, sometimes with an aura of distrust, before breaking down to form the international English-speaking society that characterizes the Riviera today. Somerset Maugham is perhaps the best representative of this slow process of

intermixing. English by nationality but idolized by the Americans, he was one of the most popular authors in Hollywood. His works gave rise to over fifty films, from *The Divorcee*, starring Ethel Barrymore, in 1919, to *Of Human Bondage* in 1964, with Kim Novak. Stars from Greta Garbo to Gene Tierney acted in films adapted from his books. Despite all this flattering attention, Somerset Maugham was able to keep a cool head, noting that the Côte d'Azur was becoming a sunny place for some rather shady characters. He was the first to write about the reality of this Anglo-American circle on the coast, again in *The Razor's Edge*, which describes the new society that the author himself was helping to shape. The English narrator, living in St.-Jean-Cap-Ferrat, follows the adventures of a group of young Americans he had met in Chicago years before.

The event that brought the new society into sharp focus was the reception held at the Château Horizon, in Cap d'Antibes, for the marriage of Ali Kahn and the queen of Hollywood, Rita Hayworth, in 1947. We note with some irony that the couple was officially married at the town hall in Vallauris by a mayor representing the French Communist Party. Among the hundreds of guests immortalized by crowds of eager photographers were Elsa Maxwell, Darryl Zanuck, and Lady Hemsley, the sister of the British ambassador. Elsa Maxwell stole the show. She was as huge as she was sharp-tongued, and her

"TO CATCH A THIEF"
Starring CARY GRANT and GRACE KELLY
with Jessie Royce Landis · John Williams
Alfred Hitchcock Production · Technicolor® · A Paramount Re-release

Copyright 1954 by Paramount Pictures Corporation. Per-
mission granted for newspaper and magazine reproduction
when given credit to Paramount Pictures Corporation.
(Made in U.S.A.)

11511-21

Film poster for *To Catch a Thief*, directed by
Alfred Hitchcock and starring Grace Kelly,
which was shot on the Riviera. The poster shows a view
of Monaco, where Grace was later to become princess.

Alfred Hitchcock and Grace Kelly
during the filming of *To Catch a Thief.*

**La Torre Clementina, in Cap
Martin,** a real symbol of life on the Côte
d'Azur. It is one of the few grand villas to
preserve the splendors of its heyday.

uproarious gossip columns and features in cinema
magazines and radio programs were wildly popular.
She was a regular visitor to the Riviera, spending
her holidays for years with one of her friends, Miss
Gordon, near Grasse, and had in fact introduced the
happy couple to each other, on the terrace of the
Masque de Fer restaurant at the Palm Beach casino.
The wedding of a man revered by millions as the
son of God to the most beautiful girl in the world
was one of the biggest coups of Elsa's career, and
the event created one of the biggest traffic jams in
the history of the Riviera.

Alfred Hitchcock — a symbol of the successful
crossover from England to America — gave his
personal vision of the enduring fascination for what
he called the most beautiful place in the world. His
film *To Catch a Thief* introduced his star Grace Kelly
both to the Riviera and to her future husband,
Prince Rainier of Monaco. Aristotle Onassis, who
owned vast tracts of the coast as well as the casino

and most of the major hotels, was very keen for the
prince to marry a Hollywood star as a publicity
stunt. The name of Marilyn Monroe was in the air
for a while, but fate had other plans. In one
memorable scene of the film, Grace Kelly parks her
car on the hillside above Monaco, turns to Cary
Grant, telling him that the view is one of the
loveliest in the world. Little did she suspect that one
day, she would be its princess. Even though things
did not quite run according to his plan, Aristotle
Onassis was right about one thing. The marriage of
Rainier and Grace signaled a new lease of life for
the tiny principality perched on the rocks
overlooking the Mediterranean. American money
soon flowed in, and Monaco underwent an
astonishing period of development, making it the
fiscal paradise it is today.

Anthony Burgess, Lawrence Durrell, Kirk
Douglas — who married a young local girl — were just
some of the famous names to come to the Riviera

The Villa Fiorentina in St.-Jean-Cap-Ferrat,
and its superb garden, designed by the famous
landscape gardener Roderick Cameron. Liz Taylor
and Richard Burton rented the villa as a hideaway.

An original design for the Villa Fiorentina in St.-Jean-Cap-Ferrat.

A painting of the
Villa Fiorentina on
its exceptional site at
Pointe St.-Hospice.
The building has now
been subdivided into
several properties.
Clos Fiorentina was
later bought by Hubert
de Givenchy.

for a few weeks, a few months, or even a few years.
They spent their time in fabulous gardens left by the
wealthy British visitors of the early years of the
century, in villas restored and redecorated by
millionaires from California, in Broom's nightclub in
Cannes (the name was derived from Lord Brougham,
the first "patron saint" of the Riviera). Some of the
visitors were so charmed that they bought their own
villa—David Niven purchased the Villa Lo Scoglietto,
and Gregory Peck the Villa La Doma in St.-Jean-
Cap-Ferrat—or even their own hotel, like the Powell
family, who took over the Voile d'Or. The hotel was
managed for a time by Michael Powell, the English-
born Hollywood director of films such as *The Tales of
Hoffmann* and *The Red Shoes*, and father of the actor
Robert Powell. The Voile d'Or was a favorite with
many British actors, such as Alec Guinness, Jack
Hawkins, and Dirk Bogarde.

In this melting-pot of Anglo-American society
some places have now become genuine emblems of
this blend of influences, like the Villa La Torre
Clementina, in the very British enclave of Cap
Martin, but restored by the American John Bolt in
the 1980s, or La Fiorentina in St.-Jean-Cap-Ferrat.
After the Second World War, Roderick Cameron,
author of *The Golden Riviera*, decided to redesign the
gardens of the property belonging to his mother, the
Countess Kenmare. The countess, who had enjoyed

an extravagant lifestyle on the Riviera, was the
owner of La Fiorentina, a huge domain on the far
tip of the cape, at Saint Hospice, and a smaller, more
modest residence, the Clos Fiorentina. The grounds
had been landscaped at the beginning of the century
by Ferdinand Bac, the grandson of Jérôme
Napoleon, but there were now many changes to be
made. Roderick Cameron played down the
theatrical, stagy aspect of the grounds, creating two
long, narrow canals as well as a number of footpaths.
He had the idea, since widely copied, of
whitewashing the trunks of the orange trees for a
decorative effect. The result was a subtle blend of
the spectacular, like the famous alley of cypress trees
leading down to the sea, and the intimate, with
walled and secret gardens within the main grounds.
Word of the garden's beauty spread around the
world. Roderick Cameron was the perfect English
gentleman, but welcomed Hollywood to his domain:
Greta Garbo and Liz Taylor and Richard Burton
rented the property several times. Today, the Clos
Fiorentina belongs to Hubert de Givenchy, who has
hired Roderick Cameron's original gardener to
restore the gardens to the way they were at the
height of their beauty. Eccentric English gentlemen,
art-loving Americans, and artistic souls of all
nationalities found their little Eden, here in this
south-eastern corner of France.

Cap d'Antibes. The gardens of the Villa Eilenroc.

To the Present

The works of Edith Wharton have a great deal in common with the Riviera. Edith Wharton, sharp-eyed critic of the excesses of luxury, which all too often hide the fear of a spiritual emptiness, found on the Côte d'Azur a world that was as familiar to her as her own childhood. She chose to live a life of semi-retirement, as if she needed, for her own powers of concentration, to be at once in the center of things, and a cold-eyed witness watching the action from her position on the bounds.

Today, the Riviera is a much more accessible place. Ordinary holidaymakers are free to stroll on the paths along the coastline, sometimes crossing one of the gardens that reach down to the sea, occasionally finding a dilapidated Byzantine pergola with peeling paint, a Moorish folly, a Scottish castle with crumbling walls, or seventy-year-old antique ruins—relics of the grandeur and decadence of a golden age now past, fitting scenery for one of Edith Wharton's own novels.

And yet—although some of these magnificent follies have been transformed into apartment

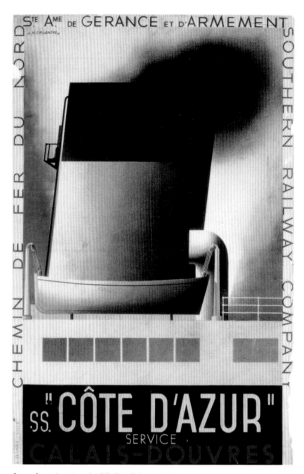

A poster advertises the *S.S. Côte d'Azur* service, operating between England and France.

blocks, or even demolished altogether, many still stand proud, cherished homes for another generation of wealthy playboys and stars. These private kingdoms are as inaccessible as ever to the ordinary tourist, but the age of grand receptions lasting three days is over: nowadays, the Riviera is a much more clandestine place. The elite has changed. Then, the villas belonged to princes and bankers; today their owners are as likely to be rock stars and top models. As the son of Somerset Maugham's gardener has said, "Before, the fortunes were public knowledge, and doors were open. Today, the fortunes are secret, and the doors are closed." There are still plenty of British and American billionaires with fabulous homes all along the coast, but nowadays the watchword is discretion. The Jazz Festival

founded in Antibes in 1960 has continued to bring the rich and famous to these shores, and Roger Moore, Elton John, Tina Turner, and George Michael all have homes here. In fact, Tina Turner apparently made an offer to the Institut de France for the Villa Kerylos, before deciding to take inspiration from it for her own design. The new generation of stars has moved a few miles along the coast, and the new hot spot is St. Tropez, a town that used to be an exclusively French secret.

Edith Wharton never went to St. Tropez, but it is certain that it would have given her a lot to write about. She died in 1937, after suffering a stroke on the annual drive back to Paris from Hyères. She is buried in her adopted country, near the grave of her dear friend Walter Berry.

"Sunshine All Year Round On The Côte d'Azur,"
advertising poster for a train company, designed by Roger Broders.

La Côte d'Azur

bibliography

Philippe Alexandre and Béatrice de l'Aulnoit, *Victoria, la Dernière Reine*. Robert Laffont, 2000.

Christian Arthaud and Eric L. Paul, *La Côte d'Azur des Ecrivains*. Édisud 1999.

Richard Balducci, *Les Princesses de Paris, l'âge d'or des cocottes*. Hors Collection, 1994.

Charles Bilas and Lucien Rosso, *French Riviera: The 20s and 30s*. Vilo International, 1999.

Mary Blume, *Cote d'Azur: Inventing the French Riviera*. Thames & Hudson,1994.

Jean Bresson, *Ces Demeures qui ont fait Cannes*. Le Rocher, 1975.

Jan Brusse, *Voici la Côte d'Azur*. Flammarion, 1964.

Alain Decaux, *Les Heures brillantes de la Côte d'Azur*. Librairie académique, Perrin, 1964.

F. Scott Fitzgerald, *Tender Is the Night*. Scribner Classics, 1996.

Albert Flament, *La Côte d'Azur*. Flammarion, 1932.

Henri Gault and Christian Millan, *Guide de la Côte d'Azur*. Juillard, 1968.

Didier Gayraud, *Villefranche sur Mer, Beaulieu sur Mer, Saint Jean Cap Ferrat*. Collection Le Temps Retrouvé. Equinoxe, 1998.

Michel Georges-Michel, *Un demi-siècle de Gloires théâtrales*. Editions André Bonne, 1950.

Guide du Syndicat d'Initiative de Nice, 1959.

Gourmet Guide. London, 1908.

Guide Provence/Côte d'Azur. Gallimard, 2000.

Louisa Jones, *Gardens of the French Riviera*. Flammarion, 2002.

Hugues de La Touche, *Sur les pas de Jean Cocteau*. Editions Rom 1998.

Pierre Leprohon, *Côte d'Azur*. Editions Hermès, 1967.

R.W.B. Lewis, *Edith Wharton: A Biography*. Fromm, 1985.

Diane de Margerie, *Edith Wharton*. Flammarion, 2000.

W. Somerset Maugham, *The Razor's Edge*. Penguin 20th Century Classics, 1992.

Michelin Green Guide: French Riviera. Michelin Travel Publications, 2001.

Vivian Russell, *Edith Wharton's Italian Gardens*. Bulfinch Press, 1998.

Pierre Schneider, *Matisse*. Rizzoli, 1984.

Hugo Vickers, *The Private World of the Duke and Duchess of Windsor*. Abbeville Press, 1996.

Marc Walter, *Palaces et Grands Hôtels d'Europe*. Flammarion, 1984.

Edith Wharton, *A Backward Glance: An Autobiography*. Touchstone, 1998.

picture credits